Praise for Gold, the Real B
Sources of Monetary

M000273250

"In this book, preeminent monetary historians Tom Humphrey and Richard Timberlake persuasively document the baneful effects of a well-intentioned but hopelessly flawed economic idea—the Real Bills Doctrine. Conceived as a principle for achieving sustainable noninflationary monetary conditions by tying note issue to a subset of bank loans, those driven by 'real' transactions as opposed to 'speculative purposes,' it guided the original design and early policy decisions of the Federal Reserve. The resulting preoccupation with credit market conditions led Fed leadership to dramatically misread signals after 1929 and effectively tighten monetary policy just as the U.S. economy began contracting at the onset of the Great Depression. The authors thus demonstrate the neglected contribution of bad economic ideas to the greatest economic contraction of the 20th century. Unfortunately, remnants of the Real Bills Doctrine live on today, as seen in central bankers' ruminations about 'excessive lending' and 'macroprudential policy.' If you've ever wondered about the historical origins and intellectual foundations of such rhetoric, you will be interested in this fascinating book."

—JEFFREY LACKER, former president and CEO of
the Federal Reserve Bank of Richmond

"It certainly was not adherence to any kind of gold standard that caused the [Great Depression]. If anything, it was the lack of adherence that did. Had either we or France adhered to the gold standard, the money supply in the United States, France, and other countries on the gold standard would have increased substantially.... [Tom Humphrey and Dick Timberlake's] emphasis of the Real Bills Doctrine complements in an important way Anna [Schwartz] and my analysis of why Fed policy was so 'inept.' We stressed and discussed at great length the shift of power in the System. We did not emphasize, as in hindsight... we should have, the widespread belief in the Real Bills Doctrine on the part of those to whom the power shifted."

—MILTON FRIEDMAN, recipient of the 1976 Nobel Prize in Economic Sciences

"In my opinion, this is the most important book written on the Great Depression since Friedman and Schwartz published their *Monetary History of the United States*. In originality and significance, I know of no other book that comes close to this book in explaining why U.S. monetary policy during the Depression allowed a financial panic, not significantly different from the Panic of 1907, to cripple the banking system, destroy a third of the money supply, and cause the most traumatic economic downturn in our history.

Humphrey and Timberlake provide clear and convincing arguments and evidence that the Gold Standard was not a cause or even a contributing factor in producing the Great Depression in the United States. Of greater significance, in my opinion, the book points to an obscure and largely forgotten theory, the Real Bills Doctrine, as the culprit for the failure of the Federal Reserve Bank to respond to the collapse of the money supply, which turned a financial panic into a Great Depression. That failure changed the history of America and its system of government.

Except for a few monetary historians no one today even remembers the Real Bills Doctrine or the sway it held over economic thinking, despite the fact that it had been discredited over and over again for 225 years. By the time that the Financial Panic of 1929 occurred, the majority of the members of the Fed leadership believed that if banks made short-term loans on the basis of real collateral or real bills, backed by real economic activity in industry and agriculture, the money supply was self-regulating and inherently stable, even without the gold standard. This doctrine led the Federal Reserve Bank to stand by and watch one-third of the banks in the country go broke and the money supply fall faster than prices. An irrational distaste for speculation led the Fed to end its lending to banks that made loans for the purpose of investing in stocks and bonds, needlessly contributing to bank failures and a collapse in the money supply. It was the Real Bills Doctrine, which Senator Carter Glass had espoused 20 years before the Great Depression, that led to the Glass-Steagall Act of 1933, which artificially narrowed the scope of American banking for almost 70 years.

I strongly recommend this book to anyone who seeks to understand the economic history of America."

—PHIL GRAMM, economist and former chairman of the Senate Banking Committee

GOLD, THE REAL BILLS DOCTRINE, AND THE FED

GOLD, THE REAL BILLS DOCTRINE, AND THE FED

SOURCES OF MONETARY DISORDER
·············· 1922–1938 ···············

THOMAS M. HUMPHREY

RICHARD H. TIMBERLAKE

CATO INSTITUTE

eBook ISBN: 978-1-948647-13-7
Paperback ISBN: 978-1-948647-12-0
Hardback ISBN: 978-1-948647-55-7

Library of Congress Cataloging-in-Publication Data available.

Printed in the United States of America

Cover design: Faceout Designs

Cato Institute
1000 Massachusetts Ave., N.W.
Washington, D.C. 20001
www.cato.org

To Mitzi and Hildegard, Our Forever Helpmates

CONTENTS

LIST OF ILLUSTRATIONS

Figures

Tables

Preface

We have approached the writing of this account of the Real Bills Doctrine's contribution to monetary instability in the 1920s and 1930s with a few thoughts in mind. First, it seemed to be a readily available topic that had never been thoroughly discussed, although one that both of us had explored in connection with other banking research. Second, it had an aura of drama about it, since that doctrine had figured in many of the banking controversies of the 19th and early 20th centuries, especially in England and the United States. Third, it looked like it had enough substance to be a book.

At the same time, we wondered why other researchers had not picked up such an obvious subject and run with it. It seemed too easy—like a $100 bill that no one had claimed, lying on the sidewalk. Although we have since learned that some other economists know about the doctrine's former prominence, none of them recognized just how important it was in the period we emphasize.

We have also discovered—much to our surprise—that the Real Bills Doctrine is not by itself either a stabilizing or a destabilizing force. Its stability depends on the financial environment in which it functions; it cannot exist in a monetary vacuum. It is metastable, picking up whatever characteristic is built into current monetary policy. To label it "inherently unstable" is simply incorrect.

What, though, is the importance of analyzing an economic doctrine and the economic policies it fostered almost a century ago? The doctrine proper has for the most part been consigned to the dustbin of history. But the Great Contraction and Depression of 1929–1941, to which the doctrine inadvertently contributed, continues to be discussed and often misinterpreted. So the answer is obvious. It is a history that must be examined. Otherwise, to paraphrase the philosopher George Santayana, Those who cannot, or will not, learn from this history are doomed to repeat it.

Today's scholars must have at their disposal accurate accounts of the past to derive credible policies for the present. Our book provides new evidence, not only for the Great Contraction and Great Depression, but also for the stable price level policy of Benjamin Strong that preceded them. We also document the innocence of the gold standard for many of the monetary troubles of the period, and we present an empirical analysis to explain the bungling disaster of the recession-within-a-depression of 1937. Each of these episodes had its own special variables promoting and aggravating it; the anti-speculative element of the Real Bills Doctrine was only the first and most severe.

Acknowledgments

We begin by thanking most especially George Selgin, James Dorn, Tom Clougherty, and Tyler Whirty, our indefatigable editors at the Cato Institute, for their knowledge, insights, and patience with our text. Long ago, one of us had a teacher, Lloyd W. Mints at the University of Chicago, who not only knew about the Real Bills Doctrine, but formally introduced it to the economics profession. Mints was also very critical of it.

In contrast to Mints, another professional friend, Alfred Bornemann, who believed wholeheartedly in the doctrine, wrote a doctoral thesis on its major academic proponent, J. Laurence Laughlin. Bornemann's history of Laughlin and early 20th-century proponents of the doctrine contributed much to our understanding. Both Mints's criticism and Bornemann's acceptance of the doctrine reflected each economist's interpretation of the Federal Reserve Act and what it implied the Fed could and should do about monetary policy.

Much of our account has leaned heavily on Milton Friedman and Anna Schwartz's *A Monetary History of the United States, 1867–1960* (Princeton University Press, 1963), for informing us of the institutional framework in which the doctrine flourished. We hope we have added a critical supplement to their incomparable work on what has happened to the U.S. monetary system since the Civil War. Their account of the Great Depression–Contraction, because of its credibility, has been especially helpful.

We also thank Jeff Lacker, recently retired president of the Federal Reserve Bank of Richmond, and Robert Hetzel, also just retired from the same institution, for their encouraging comments. We gave an earlier version of the book to Dr. Albert Santora (anesthesiologist) for a layman's comments. He reported that our book would not put readers to sleep.

We also have some family members to thank for critical technical assistance: Humphrey's granddaughter, Isabel Scarpino, for preparing the book's sole diagram and Timberlake's youngest son, Tommy, for much help in preparing the several tables of data on money stocks, gold, and employment.

Finally, we want to thank our longtime and enduring helpmates, Mitzi and Hildegard. To them we also dedicate this book.

Introduction

From 1929 to mid-1933, the United States suffered an unprecedented monetary collapse. The money stock declined by 33 percent, as did the price level. The unemployment rate rose to 24 percent of the workforce, while gross national product fell by nearly a third. Almost 40 percent of the country's 23,000 commercial banks failed. In their magisterial *A Monetary History of the United States*, Milton Friedman and Anna Schwartz (1963) called this calamitous episode "The Great Contraction." The economic devastation it caused was so severe, and the policy response to it was so inept, that contraction soon gave way to depression. The United States would not escape its Great Depression until 1941.

How could such a disaster have happened? What caused the Great Contraction of 1929–1933, and why were Federal Reserve policymakers unable to respond effectively to it? Many observers—both at the time and to this day—have blamed the gold standard for the contraction and the depression that followed it. The gold standard's many critics regard it as an antiquated institution that fatally tied the hands of authorities in the 1930s and prevented them from saving the U.S. economy from disaster.

In reality, however, no account of events in the United States in the 1920s and 1930s could be further from the truth. A dispassionate observer could hardly imagine that a naturally occurring gold money, with a long history of disciplined and orderly acceptance and operation behind it, could suddenly in the few years between 1929 and 1933 have initiated and prolonged a worldwide depression of such magnitude. It simply does not make sense. For one thing, the operational gold standard, according to which the movement of gold into and out of the United States automatically determined the economy's stock of common money (i.e., banknotes and deposits), ended forever when the United States became a belligerent in World War I. What replaced it was a pseudo–gold standard *managed* by the Federal Reserve System (the Fed). That institution's founding legislation, the Federal Reserve Act of 1913, required Federal Reserve banks to maintain minimum gold reserves against their issues of Federal Reserve note currency and their holdings of reserve balances for member banks. Indeed, during the years of the Great Contraction, Federal Reserve officials frequently suggested that they were constrained by the "limited" quantity of monetary gold reserves available.

This view, however, ignores the fact that the Federal Reserve Act gave the Fed Board of Governors complete statutory power to abolish all gold reserve requirements in the event of an emergency. That is, *all* the Fed banks' gold reserves, both "required" and "excess," were available for any necessary redemptions. In addition, no shortage of monetary gold appeared in Fed banks during the Great Contraction. By mid-1931, Federal Reserve banks had more than double the legally required gold reserves. As late as early March 1933, Federal Reserve banks collectively still held more gold than they had had in 1929. And although that month witnessed a run on gold that ultimately precipitated the National Bank Holiday, only the New York Federal Reserve Bank was in danger of breaching its gold reserve requirement. The Federal Reserve System as a whole still had a gold surplus of $100 billion.

Had the Federal Reserve System wanted to, it could easily have followed Walter Bagehot's famous rules for last-resort lending throughout the Great Contraction period, using all of its gold if necessary to satisfy any panic-inspired demand for reserves. The monetary contraction and banking collapse that plunged the United States into depression and eventually led to the Bank Holiday need never have happened. What explains the Fed's inaction? What could have made the 12 Federal Reserve banks and the Fed Board in Washington completely inactive as the financial system fell apart around them? Answering that question is the chief concern of this book. Our contention is that a variant of a now-forgotten monetary theory—most commonly known as the "Real Bills Doctrine"—played a central, even determining role in bringing this economic disaster to pass. It is the "smoking gun" researchers have been seeking—and overlooking—in their efforts to identify the Great Depression's major cause.

Adhering to the Real Bills Doctrine also caused the Fed Board to misjudge the ease or tightness of its credit and monetary policies in the late 1920s and early 1930s. Policymakers argued that their policy stance was remarkably easy, when the best indicators at their disposal—the money stock, the price level, and real interest rates—were actually showing the opposite, and that monetary policy was far too tight. The Fed's consequent inaction turned what might otherwise have been a mild recession into an unparalleled depression.

The Great Contraction took hold soon after and expanded into the Great Depression in 1933. Our story continues with the Roosevelt administration's "war on gold" and the Banking Act of 1935, which together drew a curtain on the prominence of the Real Bills Doctrine as a guiding factor in U.S. monetary policy. The ugly recession of 1937–1938—a clear blunder by the Federal Reserve and U.S. Treasury—offers a fitting conclusion to this depressing tale.

We begin, however, with an explanation of the emergence and meaning of the Real Bills Doctrine and its relationship to the gold standard, and an examination of its role in the commercial banking sector of the day.

$$\left(1 \right)$$

REAL BILLS, BANKS, AND GOLD

During the particular eras in which the Real Bills Doctrine flourished as a major banking and monetary principle, gold currencies provided a reserve base for notes and deposits created by fractional reserve commercial banks.[1] In turn, those commercial banknotes[2] and deposits made up most of the money in common use.

Commercial banks often furnished new money by means of loans secured by borrowers' IOUs—paper claims to their goods in the process of production. When banks made such loans, they accepted a "real bill" as an asset in their portfolios and created a corresponding liability—a bank deposit—on their balance sheet. The bank furnished the new demand deposit money to the borrower who was manufacturing real goods or services. Such money, when paid out to the owners of factor inputs hired to fabricate the finished goods, was, ideally, enough to provide for the purchase of those goods when they were marketed.

The Real Bills Doctrine is rooted in this system of money creation. It states that money can never be excessive or deficient when issued in the form of loans against short-term, self-liquidating commercial bills arising from real transactions in goods and services. So long as bankers lend only at short term on goods that will become finished and marketed in 30, 60, or 90 days, the money stock will be secured by and

---

[1] For simplicity's sake, we use only "gold" in the following exposition. However, both gold and silver were used extensively in various monetary systems throughout the commercial world. Both were acceptable as legal tender in the Constitution of the United States. Silver, however, became too plentiful in the 19th century and, therefore, lost its secular constancy of real value (Timberlake 1993: 146–83). The issues of government legal tender paper money ("greenbacks") during the Civil War added to the moneys that constituted the "monetary base" of the era.

[2] Until 1866, at the end of the Civil War in the United States, banks mostly used their own notes to finance the loans they made to borrowers. A federal law in that year prohibited the issue of these banknote currencies, forcing commercial banks to use checkbook money to finance the loans—real bills—they made after June 1867 (Timberlake 2013: 79–85). National banks were still permitted to issue a limited amount of banknotes.

will automatically vary with real production, so that real output will be matched by just enough money to purchase it at existing prices.

To put it another way, inflationary and deflationary over- and under-issue are impossible provided that money is issued by way of loans made to finance real transactions.[3] That, at least, is the theory behind the Real Bills Doctrine.

THE REAL BILLS DOCTRINE IN COMMERCIAL BANKING

The Real Bills Doctrine was, first and foremost, an important norm of commercial banking theory and practice. It functioned as a rule for "sound" banking—a good-conduct code for bankers purporting to gear the new bank money to real production by means of the short-term commercial bill of exchange.

Because the real bills arising from bank loans and discounts reflected the presence of real goods and services, bankers regarded the bills in their portfolios as a quasi-reserve against the notes or deposits that accompanied their issue. The bills, though not gold, would very soon be paid off as they matured, and the bank money ("credit") that the bills had initiated would be canceled. Therefore, it seemed to advocates of the Real Bills Doctrine that real bills legitimately "monetized" the goods and services whose production they financed.

Figure 1 shows a schematic balance sheet for a typical "real bills bank" and illustrates how gold and real bills would appear in such a banking system.

The bank begins with the original gold deposits of its stockholders, who have a residual claim on the bank's net earnings—or profits—derived from the interest payments made on loans issued by the bank. The new real bills that the bank has acquired as collateral,

---

[3] One thing the Real Bills Doctrine most assuredly is not is the theory presented under that name by Sargent and Wallace in their well-known article, "The Real-Bills Doctrine versus the Quantity Theory: A Reconsideration." Conflating real bills with free banking, Sargent and Wallace (1982) claim that such regimes are socially and economically optimal despite their tendency to produce monetary and price level instability/indeterminacy. In his authoritative critique of the Sargent-Wallace paper, David Laidler (1984) notes that regardless of the merits of their model, it nevertheless reaches "conclusions . . . that would have been anathema to [the doctrine's 18th and 19th century] proponents" and that "what they [Sargent and Wallace] refer to as the real bills doctrine is not the doctrine" as traditionally understood. Such are the perils of labeling new theories with the names of old doctrines when the two differ.

FIGURE 1

Balance Sheet for a Real Bills Bank

ASSETS		LIABILITIES	
Bank loans (real bills)	(+$90)	Banknotes and bank deposits	(+$90)
Gold reserves	(+$10)	Original gold deposit	(+$10)

Note: Gold reserve ratio = 10 percent; real bills "reserve" ratio = 90 percent.

in enabling producers to finance the production of goods, will soon
have to be paid off. But in the meantime, the production of the goods
that the real bills are financing is completed, and the goods are sold
in markets. From the sales receipts, the real bills borrowers then
pay off the bank, canceling their real bills obligations. At the same
time, the bank may be making loans to new real bills borrowers, who
wish to do the same thing. The new bank deposits, which are simply
demand-deposit money to the credit of bank depositors, continue to
exist, as the dynamic credit process continues. If new gold is deposited, as happens gradually with a functioning gold standard, this typical bank will realize additional gold deposits and be able to expand
slightly its credit-creating activities.

THE ROLE OF THE GOLD STANDARD

Long before the appearance of the Real Bills Doctrine, metallic gold
and silver moneys had come into common use in Europe, Asia, and the
Americas. Both gold and silver, but especially gold, had many valuable monetary properties: both are universally recognizable, durable,
portable, and divisible, and their production is limited enough to keep
their long-run relative value with all other economic goods and services virtually constant (see Jastram 1977). Gold also had popular recognition and understanding. "Everybody" knew that more gold meant
more money, and vice versa.

Gold money, however, is not the same thing as a gold standard. Gold money evolved over centuries as the most enduring
medium that would fulfill the functions of a stable medium of
exchange. A gold *standard*, on the other hand, requires political

3

acceptance: some Exchequer, Congress, or Treasury Department must stipulate that a particular quantity of gold equals some precise quantity of dollars,[4] and this price must be fixed by law no matter what the state of the Union, business conditions, who is president, or any other public problem. The gold standard, in this sense, became widespread between the 17th and 19th centuries (De Cecco 1992: 260–67).[5]

As long as the government and all households and businesses obey the law, the gold standard is self-regulating through the market system.[6] The fact that money appears in all markets—and is used to express the prices of all goods and services—means that the prices of those goods and services, by inversion, also define the value of the money unit. In a gold standard system all common money—paper banknotes or bank checks—can be converted into gold, and, therefore, the same market activity that determines the values of all goods and services also determines the real value of common money and gold.[7] If the prices of goods in terms of money go up, the price of money—including the price of gold—in terms of the goods and services it can purchase must decline.

This relationship reflects both the supplies and demands for goods and services and the demands and supplies for money, including gold. Everybody is working and buying and selling goods and services in those markets, and everybody hopes to improve his or her personal wealth and income.

---

[4] In the United States, Congress had the constitutional authority for this action under Article 1, Section 8, for both gold and silver, with the additional power to "regulate the value thereof"—meaning to *adjust* the prices of either gold or silver so as to keep both metals in circulation (Timberlake 2013: 35–39).

[5] For thorough and accurate treatments of the gold standard in the United States, see Selgin (2017: 177–210) and White (2008).

[6] This condition was fulfilled in the United States until 1862, when, under the pressure of the Civil War, Congress initiated the greenback currency. For an account of this action and its ramifications, see Timberlake (2013: chaps. 9–13).

[7] Common money includes any medium of exchange that can be spent, and is spent, to clear purchases and sales of goods and services. This definition limits the items that can be used as money to hand-to-hand currency (coin and paper money) and bank deposits subject to check—that is, checkbook money balances.

REAL BILLS, BANKS, AND GOLD

As Marcello De Cecco (1992: 260–61) puts it, a gold standard money freed the economic world from the uncertainties induced by ambitious regents

> who exercised or usurped monetary sovereignty. A pure metallic money would be subject to the same laws of value to which other commodities were subject; its demand and supply would be determined strictly by the needs of trade. . . . [Gold money] would not disturb the functioning of economic laws, since it obeyed those laws.

THE REAL BILLS DOCTRINE'S FATAL FLAWS

The Real Bills Doctrine came into existence some 300 years ago as a complementary postulate to the gold standard. Gold provided commercial banks with a reserve base, and the Real Bills Doctrine guided their loan-making activities. Boiled down to its essentials, the idea was that the "right" quantity of money would be created if bank credit (in the form of loans to businesses) was tied to output (in the form of goods in the process of production). The Real Bills Doctrine put this idea into practice by having banks lend against "real bills"—commercial paper representing claims to the goods being produced—so that the money stock would vary according to the needs of trade.

Though popular with bankers and superficially plausible,[8] the Real Bills Doctrine was flawed from the very start. It failed to distinguish nominal from real output. It linked one nominal variable, the money stock, with another nominal variable, the dollar volume of commercial paper. This characteristic meant that the Real Bills Doctrine could not, by itself, establish any effective limits on either money or prices. Once disturbed by disequilibrating shocks, both the quantity of money and money prices could rise or fall unchecked.

---

[8] Joseph Schumpeter (1954: 730) attributed the doctrine's popularity to its tendency to make bankers look good, by featuring them as social benefactors. He argued that the Real Bills Doctrine features the real bills banker as "the helpmate of commodity trade, who offers his money to satisfy the needs of business but does not force it upon business [and] who has nothing to do with price fluctuations, and overtrading." Bankers naturally "like to see themselves in this light."

To illustrate this shortcoming of the Real Bills Doctrine, imagine that a random shock from outside the monetary system sets prices rising. (The same reasoning applies in reverse to price declines.) Such rising prices require an ever-growing volume of loans just to finance the same level of real transactions. According to the Real Bills Doctrine, these loans are granted and the stock of money therefore expands. The monetary expansion may further raise prices, thereby justifying additional monetary expansion, leading to still higher prices and so on in a never-ending inflationary spiral. In this case, price inflation may induce the very monetary expansion necessary to perpetuate it, and the real bills criterion provides no effective limit either to the price level or to the quantity of money.[9]

THE DECLINE OF THE GOLD STANDARD

It is important to understand that the type of volatility outlined above could not happen under a properly functioning gold standard, nor any other *constrained* monetary system. The limited amount of gold, which under a gold standard has a fixed legal dollar price, is the base for creating the money stock and, therefore, the general price level. Banks' gold reserves change only slowly. If the quantity of real bills tended to generate too little money relative to what the gold standard allowed, bank reserves would become excessive, bankers would become less pessimistic, and bank credit would expand. If, on the other hand, bankers allowed too much bank credit on the basis of real bills, gold would flow out of the banking system—both domestically into cash hoards and externally into foreign banking systems—depleting bank reserves and bringing bank lending up short. Consequently, no matter how invalid the Real Bills Doctrine was as a policy for creating the "right" quantity of money, the system's fundamental commitment to a gold standard took precedence and made the monetary system stable.

---

[9] The doctrine possesses additional flaws. It has the money stock varying procyclically with prices and production rather than countercyclically as a stabilizing money stock would do. It draws a false and untenable distinction between production and speculation, with a bias against the latter. It fails to see that all production, motivated by expectation of uncertain future profit, is inherently speculative, just as speculative activity, to the extent it creates real value, is productive.

The problem, however, was that some advocates of the Real Bills Doctrine, who were blind to its flaws, believed that a real bills system could properly finance increases in real goods and at the same time effectively regulate the total volume of bank credit—even without a gold reserve base. As the chapters that follow will show, such people were able to rise to positions of power and influence as central banks came increasingly to manage the gold standard. That development enabled the transformation of the Real Bills Doctrine from a misguided but relatively innocuous banking norm to a dangerous and—ultimately—deeply damaging principle for the conduct of monetary policy.

Indeed, most of the "problems" now mistakenly attributed to a gold standard system in fact arose from the notion that some institution, such as a central bank, had to control or manage the quantity of gold that became money. Michael Bordo (1992: 269), in his extended account of the gold standard in *The New Palgrave Dictionary of Money and Finance*, states properly that, "The basic rule of the gold standard was for the monetary authority of each country to define the price of gold in terms of its currency and keep the price fixed." Further on, in his discussion of the gold standard's vicissitudes, Bordo concludes:

> The final theme in the theory of the international gold standard is the role of central banks and the "rules of the game." *At the most basic level there is no need for central banks to manage the gold standard.* All that is required is that some monetary authority be ready to maintain convertibility of national currency into gold. . . . Central banks emerged in Europe originally as government fiscal agents and then (naturally) evolved into both a banker's bank and a repository of the nation's gold reserves. . . . The gold standard came to be regarded as a managed standard—managed by central banks' use of changes in the discount rate and other policy tools to facilitate adjustment to both internal and external gold drains (Bordo 1992: 269, emphasis added).

Not only is there no "need for central banks to manage the gold standard," *but* any management of gold abrogates gold as a standard.

Bordo concludes that central banks began as ancillaries to the gold standard. In time, however, they extended their role to become institutions that served the state's fiscal excesses by controlling the quantity of money, which meant controlling the amount of gold that became common money. They would not leave the creation of such a valuable item as money to the market-based system—as a gold standard requires.

Central banks—all of them—came to manage their gold standard systems. As the degree of gold standard management increased, gold standards became less and less pure gold standards and more and more fiat money standards that furnished fiscal resources to the governments controlling them. Finally, gold no longer had any monetary properties or influence on money stocks. Rather it was collected into national treasuries as if it were an historical artifact, which it had indeed become, leaving the treasuries and central banks in full control of every economy's stock of money.

It was in precisely this context that the Real Bills Doctrine came to inspire a Federal Reserve monetary policy that would trigger the Great Contraction of 1929–1933 and then plunge the United States into a Great Depression that lasted until 1941. The evidence—the facts—that we document here completely exonerate the operational, hands-off, gold standard from responsibility for the ills of that era. The villain in the play was a variant of the Real Bills Doctrine.

(2)

THE REAL BILLS DOCTRINE IN THE HISTORY OF MONETARY THOUGHT

The concept of an output-governed currency secured by claims to real property and responding to the needs of trade has a long history. Lloyd Mints (1945), the doctrine's foremost 20th-century critic, traced the basic idea to John Law (1671–1729). It was Law who, in his *Money and Trade Considered* (1705), proposed that banknote issue be secured by and bear a fixed ratio to the market value of land, which in Law's prototypical version of the doctrine was the key representative indicator and measure of real activity. In advocating a land-collateralized note issue, Law contended four things. First, money's purchasing power should be kept stable. Second, such price stability requires limiting the note issue to the real needs of trade. Third, this limitation can be achieved by tying the note issue to the value of land (a proximate indicator of national product in economies where agriculture looms large). Fourth, linking the note issue to land's value provides an automatic check to overissue since the notes cannot exceed the value of their collateral.[1] In Law's own words:

> I . . . propose . . . to make Money of Land equal to its [land's] Value. . . . This Paper Money will keep its value [i.e., purchasing power], and there will always be as much Money as there is Occasion or Imployment [sic] for, and no more. . . . Since it is very practicable to make Land Money, it would be contrary to Reason to limit the Industry of the People, by making it depend on a Species [such as gold or silver] not in our Power . . . when we have a Species [i.e., land] of our own every way more qualified (Law 1720: 62, 75, 95).[2]

---

[1] On Law, see Mints (1945: 15–16, 18, 20, 30–32) and Fetter (1965: 7–9).

[2] Omnibus quotation cited in Fetter (1965: 7–8).

Law's statement is the origin and prototype of the idea that money cannot be inflationary if backed by sound productive assets, in this case, land.

LAW'S ERROR

Law sought a criterion that would limit monetary expansion and ensure price stability. He thought that land's value provided such a criterion. Collateralized by land, money could never be overissued because it would always be constrained by the value of the real property backing it. What he overlooked was that the market value of property contains a price component that is in fact determined by the money supply itself. With money determining the level of prices and prices in turn influencing land's value—a value that drives the money stock—the result is a two-way interaction between money and prices in which both can rise without limit. Law failed to see that monetary expansion raises prices and that rising prices, by augmenting the nominal value of land, justify further monetary expansion, leading to further price increases and so on in a cumulative inflationary spiral. The same process could just as easily happen in reverse and lead to deflation. Law did not realize that the money value of land may provide no effective limit to the money stock or prices, because both can expand or contract indefinitely.

Here is the origin of the basic fallacy of the Real Bills Doctrine: namely, the notion that one uncontrolled nominal variable (the money value of land) can be used to regulate another nominal variable (the nominal money stock), as if the mere tying of a dollar to another dollar could ever anchor the dollar's value (see Humphrey 1982).[3]

---

[3] Law's error is easily demonstrated. Assume the banknote money supply M is strictly determined by the price-times-quantity market value of land $M = pA$, where A is the number of acres in use and p is the price per acre. The price of land p is linked to the general price level P by the relative price relationship $p = aP$, where a is land's relative price in terms of the general price level as can be seen by rewriting the equation as $a = p/P$. Next make the distinctly non-Law assumption that money determines prices. Specifically, assume that because of a time lapse between the receipt and spending of cash, money determines general prices with a one-period lag $P = kM_{-1}$, where k is the coefficient linking lagged money M_{-1} to prices. Substituting the second and third expressions into the first and solving the resulting first-order difference equations (namely, equations containing variables separated from each other by discrete time lags, in this case lags of one period) for the time paths of money and prices yields $M = M_0 [kaA]^t$ and $P = P_0 [kaA]^t$, where t is time and M_0 and P_0 are given initial values of the money stock and price level, respectively. Far from limiting money and prices, the last two equations state that those variables will either rise without limit or fall to zero with the passage of time

ADAM SMITH

If Law was the first to state that banknotes vary optimally when collateralized by the value of real property, then Adam Smith (1723–1790) was among the earliest to contend that they do so when secured by short-term, self-liquidating bills of exchange. Thus, Smith shifted the emphasis from land to commercial paper as the backing for currency. Smith ([1776] 1937: 288) stated that paper money varies optimally with the needs of trade when each bank "discounts to a merchant a real bill of exchange drawn by a real creditor upon a real debtor, and which, as soon as it becomes due, is really paid by that debtor." His statement is the origin of the phrase "real bill" to denote short-term commercial paper arising from real transactions in goods and services. According to Mints (1945: 25), Smith's statement marks him as "the first thoroughgoing exponent of the real bills doctrine" in its modern form.[4]

While endorsing the doctrine, Smith managed to avoid some of its major shortcomings. He realized that the real bills criterion by itself is insufficient to prevent overissue. For that reason, he advocated specie (i.e., gold) convertibility as the ultimate constraint on the quantity of paper money. That is, he held that banks must be required by law to redeem their paper notes in specie at a fixed price on demand. Constrained by the convertibility obligation, banks, he thought, would rarely overissue. In short, he viewed specie convertibility as the overriding check to overissue. In so doing, he avoided the error of supposing that the real bills criterion, per se, provides a sufficient limitation to the note issue regardless of the monetary regime, be it paper or metallic.

David Laidler (1981: 196–97) notes that Smith also avoids the vicious circle, or dynamic instability, problem that plagues the doctrine. That problem arises when the domestic general price level that drives the money stock is itself driven by money. This price-money-price

---

(as t takes on ever-larger values 1, 2, 3, 4, etc.) depending on whether the bracketed term is greater than or less than unity. Since each element of the bracketed term is determined by different factors, it is unlikely that the product of these elements will assume its stationary value of unity. And even if it does, changes in the magnitude of the k, a, or A elements will drive their product away from unity and touch off a never-ending inflationary or deflationary process.

[4] It was Mints who, following Smith, christened the doctrine with the appellation "real bills." Before Mints, the doctrine bore other names, most prominently (1) the commercial loan theory of banking and (2) the Banking School view.

feedback loop may enable runaway inflation or deflation. But Smith severed the loop. He denied that domestic prices in open trading economies under the gold standard are money driven. Instead they are determined in world markets by the relative costs of producing gold and goods (the gold price of goods) and are then given exogenously to the open trading economy.[5] With prices predetermined and given, it follows that they are invariant with respect to the domestic note issue. The domestic money stock cannot influence them. In this way, the assumed exogenous determination of general prices in an open national economy breaks the vicious circle of inflation and money growth besetting conventional versions of the doctrine. It renders Smith's treatment immune to the problem of dynamic instability.

Finally, Smith demonstrated that a nation's money indeed can be output determined within limits in *convertible* currency (gold standard) regimes. In so doing, he showed how the doctrine sheds its error under such regimes. With the gold standard pinning down the individual nation's price level in the price-times-quantity (PQ) nominal value of output, money is free to move with the real output component (Q) alone just as the doctrine intends. Even so, money under a real bills system still behaves pro- rather than countercyclically, rising and falling with real activity to underwrite, amplify, and lengthen cyclical booms and depressions. Smith's convertibility feature cannot resolve this shortcoming.

THE ANTI-BULLIONISTS (EARLY 1800S)

Later writers, less astute than Adam Smith, incautiously extended the Real Bills Doctrine to regimes of currency *inconvertibility*. Chief among these writers were the anti-bullionists, who employed the doctrine to exonerate the Bank of England from the accusation that it had taken advantage of the suspension of specie convertibility to overissue the British paper pound currency during the Bank Restriction period of the Napoleonic wars.

---

[5] Specifically, the general price level P, or dollar price of goods, is by definition the multiplicative product of the fixed official dollar mint price of gold G and the world gold price of goods W, or $P=GW$. Given the fixed official mint price of gold G, the world gold price of goods W determines the domestic general price level P.

The anti-bullionists adhered to the Real Bills Doctrine in its crudest, most uncompromising form. They maintained that the doctrine, *by itself,* provided a sufficient safeguard to prevent overissue even under inconvertibility. They argued that even an inconvertible paper currency could not be issued to excess as long as it was issued only upon the discount of sound, short-term commercial bills. Two considerations, they claimed, ensured that a currency backed by real bills could never be oversupplied. First, being geared to real transactions, the quantity of currency could never exceed the real demand for it. In the words of Bernard Corry (1962: 75), a modern student of the Bank Restriction period:

> Bank paper issued against the genuine "needs of trade"—that is against real security—could never become "excessive." Such issues could never be the active factor in any price rise because if they were the equivalent of real security they would only be meeting a demand for credit which was already in existence: hence—according to this view—bank credit met the needs of trade and did nothing to create those needs.

In other words, the supply of real product generates just enough money to purchase it at existing prices. Second, since no rational person would borrow at interest money not needed, banks could not force an excess issue on the market. Any temporary excess issue would immediately be returned to the banks to pay off costly loans. In short, interest-minimization considerations would ensure that any excess notes would quickly be retired from circulation.

The anti-bullionists used these arguments to defend the Bank of England against the charge that it had caused inflation. The bank, they said, was blameless since it had restricted its issues to real bills of exchange and therefore had merely responded to the real needs of trade. The bank could not possibly be the source of inflation because, by limiting its advances to commercial paper representing actual output, it had merely responded to an already existing demand for money and credit (i.e., loans) and had done nothing to create that demand.

The anti-bullionists realized, of course, that the demand for loans takes place at the going bank, or loan, rate of interest. What they overlooked was that the demand for loans does not depend solely on the loan rate of interest but rather on that rate compared with the expected rate of profit on the use of the borrowed funds. When the expected rate of profit exceeds the interest rate on the loan, the demand for loans becomes insatiable, the corresponding offer of collateral is inexhaustible, and the real bills criterion presents no bar to overissue. As discussed in the following section, that observation was a key point in Henry Thornton's criticism of the Real Bills Doctrine.

HENRY THORNTON'S CRITIQUE

If the anti-bullionists were the Bank Restriction (1797–1821) period's strongest proponents of the Real Bills Doctrine, then Henry Thornton (1760–1815)—the British banker, member of Parliament, radical religious reformer, anti-slavery activist, and all-time great monetary theorist—was by far its ablest and most penetrating critic. His devastating critique of the doctrine remains unsurpassed. In his parliamentary speeches and his 1802 classic, *An Enquiry into the Nature and Effects of the Paper Credit of Great Britain,* he denied that the real bills criterion by itself could effectively limit the banks' note issue. He upbraided the doctrine for its "error . . . of imagining that a proper limitation of banknotes may be sufficiently secured by attending merely to the nature of the security for which they are given" (Thornton [1802] 1939: 244). He then proceeded to attack the doctrine on three grounds.

First, he contended that the volume of eligible bills coming forward for discount depends not only on the quantity of goods produced, but also on the rate of turnover of those goods in the production process and the period of credit or time to maturity that bills have to run. Goods, he pointed out, may be sold a number of times, each sale giving rise to a real bill. Also, the length of time for which a given bill is customarily drawn may exceed the turnover period of the goods. Thus, depending on the number of transactions between producers in bringing goods to market and the period of credit granted, any number of bills could be generated on the alleged security of the same goods. Thornton (1939: 86) gave the following example:

> Suppose that A sells one [dollar's] worth of goods to B at six month's credit, and takes a bill at six months for it; and that B, within a month after, sells the same goods, at a like credit, to C, taking a like bill; and again, that C, after another month, sells them to D, taking a like bill, and so on.

At the end of six months, $6 of bills, all eligible for discount, would be outstanding even though only $1 worth of goods had been produced. Moreover, if the length of credit or maturity of each bill were a year rather than six months, then $12 of bills (the monthly turnover of goods remaining the same) could be issued on the security of the original $1 worth of goods-in-process.[6]

Second, Thornton argued that the Real Bills Doctrine links the nominal money stock to the nominal volume of bills, a variable that moves in step with prices and thus the money stock. In so doing, the doctrine renders the latter two variables indeterminate. It ensures that any positive shock to money and prices will, by raising the nominal value of goods in the process of production, also raise the nominal quantity of bills eligible for discount, which will lead to further increases in money and prices *ad infinitum* in a self-reinforcing inflationary spiral. Here is the flaw inherent in a doctrine that "considered security as everything and quantity [of money] as nothing" and whose proponents "forgot that there might be no bounds to the demand for paper; that the increasing quantity would contribute to the rise [in the price] of commodities: and the rise [in the price] of commodities require[s], and seem[s] to justify, a still further increase" (Thornton 1939: 342).

---

[6] More generally, the volume of bills outstanding would be $B = mGt$. Here B is the nominal quantity of bills, m their average time-to-maturity expressed as a fraction of a year, G the nominal volume of goods, and t the average number of times goods are sold and resold annually, each sale giving rise to a new real bill. Extension of m or t could, Thornton (1939: 253) wrote, result in "the greatest imaginable multiplication" of bills against a given volume of goods. Result: the quantity of money emitted against real bills would far exceed the needs of trade.

Finally, Thornton explained in great detail how pegging the loan rate of interest below the expected rate of profit on the use of the borrowed funds would set in motion a cumulative expansion of bills, loans, money, and prices. This expansion would persist as long as banks held their loan rate below the expected profit rate. Given the rate differential, money and prices would rise without limit and the real bills criterion would fail to provide the needed constraint.

He reached this conclusion via the following route. First, he argued that the demand for new loans depends primarily on the profit rate–loan rate differential:

> In order to ascertain how far the desire of obtaining loans at the bank may be expected at any time to be carried, we must enquire into the subject of the quantum of profit likely to be derived from borrowing there under the existing circumstances. This is to be judged of by considering two points: the amount, first of interest to be paid on the sum borrowed; and, secondly, of the mercantile or other gain to be obtained by the employment of the borrowed capital. . . . We may, therefore, consider this question as turning principally on a comparison of the rate of interest taken at the bank with the current rate of mercantile profit (Thornton 1939: 253–54).

Second, assume that banks accommodate new loan demands with corresponding increases in the issue of notes (and deposits) and that borrowers spend the increased issue on the full-employment level of real output, thereby raising prices proportionally with the money stock. It then follows that money and prices also rise in proportion to the interest rate differential, growing without limit as that differential persists.

Thornton stressed that the interest differential, if maintained indefinitely, produces a continuous and not merely a one-time rise in money and prices: as long as the differential persists, borrowing will continue to be profitable even at successively higher prices. The result will be more borrowing, more lending, more monetary expansion, still higher prices, and so on ad infinitum in a cumulative inflationary spiral.[7] Here in essence is the famous Wicksellian cumulative process analysis almost 100 years before Knut Wicksell himself presented it. Wicksell was totally unaware that Thornton had scooped him.[8]

On the basis of the foregoing analysis, Thornton reached two conclusions regarding the validity of the Real Bills Doctrine. First, given a profit return greater than the rate charged by the lender, the doctrine provides no bar to inflationary overissue. Second, the ineffectiveness of the real bills constraint therefore renders invalid the notion that it is safe to allow the money stock to take care of itself by adapting automatically to the needs of trade. As Thornton (1939: 254) noted

> Any supposition that it would be safe to permit the bank paper to limit itself, because this would be to take the more natural course, is, therefore, altogether erroneous. It implies that there is no occasion to advert [refer] to the rate of interest in consideration of which the bank paper is furnished, or to change that rate according to the varying circumstances of the country.

[7] Thornton's seminal analysis may be given symbolic restatement. First, suppose that business loan demands L_D expand in proportion to the profit rate–loan rate differential $(r - i)$ according to the expression

(1) $dL_D/dt = a(r - i)$

where dL_D/dt denotes the instantaneous rate of change, or time derivative of loan demands and a is the coefficient linking new loan demands to the profit rate–loan rate differential. Second, assume that the new loan demands are backed by a corresponding expansion in the volume of eligible bills B tendered for discount. Because these bills pass the real bills test, the new loan demands are accommodated with an equivalent expansion in the money stock M. In symbols,

(2) $dL_D/dt = dB/dt = dM/dt$

where L_D denotes loan demand, B the nominal volume of bills, M the money stock, and the d/dt symbol attached to each variable denotes its time derivative or rate of change. Third, suppose that prices P rise in proportion with the money stock according to the expression

(3) $dP/dt = kdM/dt$

where P is prices, M the money stock, d/dt the time derivative of its attached variable, and k the proportional relationship between price inflation and money-stock growth. Substituting equation (1) into equations (2) and (3) yields

(4) $dL_D/dt = dB/dt = dM/dt = a(r - i)$ and

(5) $dP/dt = ka(r - i)$.

These equations identify the profit rate–loan rate differential as the ultimate cause of the rise in loan demand, loan supply, eligible bills, money stock, and price level—all of which expand without limit as long as the differential persists.

[8] Wicksell was ignorant of Thornton's work until relatively late in his life, after he had already published his 1898 *Interest and Prices*. It was Wicksell's Swedish colleague David Davidson who finally told him about Thornton.

Thornton was the first to state that the real bills constraint by itself offered no effective limit to the money stock. To achieve monetary stability, other constraints such as convertibility into metallic money or direct credit rationing were required.

THE DOCTRINE AFTER THORNTON

Thornton was not alone in condemning the Real Bills Doctrine. Among his contemporaries, Lord Peter King (1804: 149) contended that when the commercial profit rate exceeds the loan rate of interest, the demand for bank loans and corresponding offer of eligible bills "may be carried to any assignable extent." Likewise, David Ricardo (1772–1823) stated that when the Bank of England charged less than the going rate of profit, "there is no amount of money which they might not lend."[9] Ricardo also denied that the needs of trade could effectively limit the note issue since, with prices rising, the needs of trade also would rise, thereby justifying extra money to purchase real output at the higher prices. Commerce at rising prices would absorb any conceivable quantity of notes and the initially excess issues would remain in circulation rather than being returned to issuing banks.

Despite these criticisms, the Real Bills Doctrine survived in 19th- and 20th-century banking circles, "scoring high," in the words of doctrinal historian Mark Blaug (1978: 56), "on the list of 'longest-lived economic fallacies.'" In England the doctrine reappeared in the middle decades of the 19th century in the celebrated Currency School/Banking School controversy over principles embodied in Prime Minister Robert Peel's Bank Act of 1844. Eager to refute the Currency School's allegation of a need for statutory control of the note issue, Banking School writers Thomas Tooke and John Fullarton posited real bills as one of three overlapping, mutually reinforcing mechanisms—the others being convertibility (of notes into specie) and reflux (the reflow of excess notes back to issuing banks)—operating singly or in combination to ensure that an unregulated money stock would take care of itself (Robbins 1968: 141).

---

[9] Ricardo ([1821] 1852: 364) cited in Viner ([1937] 1965: 150).

Of these three automatically self-correcting mechanisms, convertibility, according to Tooke and Fullarton, would see to it that any temporary excess note issue that raised British prices relative to foreign ones would be converted into gold to make cheaper purchases abroad. The resulting loss of specie would, by threatening gold reserves, force banks, including the Bank of England, to contract the note issue—thereby arresting the foreign drain and restoring money and prices to their preexisting equilibrium level. Given such monetary self-correction, convertibility alone constituted its own safeguard.

Should convertibility falter, however, the real bills mechanism would fill its place, assuring that the money stock would automatically expand and contract optimally with the needs of commerce (see Skaggs 2010).[10] And, should the real bills mechanism itself fail, a reflux mechanism would nevertheless guarantee the impossibility of note overissue. That is, overissue is ruled out because the stock of bank-issued money is demand-determined by the needs of trade. If bankers nevertheless attempt to force into circulation more notes than money holders desire, the superfluous paper will be returned to the banks either for deposit in interest-bearing accounts or to repay loans. Either way the unwanted paper will be removed from circulation, thereby sustaining monetary price level stability.

Singly or in combination, these three mechanisms—convertibility, the Real Bills Doctrine, and reflux—would, in the Banking School's

---

[10] Skaggs (2010) contends that the Banking School relied on the gold standard but not the Real Bills Doctrine to deliver a money stock sufficient for price level stability. By contrast, Fetter holds that the Banking School relied on both mechanisms, with the doctrine filling the breach when the gold standard faltered. According to Fetter (1965: 232), the Banking School held that with a convertible currency, and provided banks lend only on real bills, "the total means of payment would increase with the volume of business" such that "even though the gold supply did not increase as rapidly as production there was no danger of price declines from an inadequate monetary supply." Indeed, there is evidence that the Banking School believed real bills alone could deliver stability even in the absence of convertibility, just as the anti-bullionists had claimed. Accordingly, Banking School theorist John Fullarton could write that he had "no hesitation in professing my own adhesion to the decried doctrine of the old [anti-bullionist] Bank Directors of 1810 [at which time England was off the gold standard], 'that so long as a bank issues its notes only on the discount of good bills, at not more than sixty days' date, it cannot go wrong in issuing as many as the public will receive from it.' In that maxim, simple as it is, I verily believe, there is a nearer version of the truth, and a more profound view of the principles which govern circulation, than in any rule on the subject which since that time has been promulgated." Fullarton could never have expressed such sentiments were he not, like the cited anti-bullionist directors of the Bank of England, convinced that real bills alone could deliver stable prices without the help of gold convertibility. See Fullarton (1844: 197) cited in Fetter (1965: 193).

view, ensure that a bank-issued money stock (or at least its note component) needed no government regulation and could take care of itself.[11]

In the late 19th and early 20th centuries the doctrine reappeared
in the United States, where it formed the theoretical mainstay of
such proponents of banking reform as Charles A. Conant, A. Barton
Hepburn, J. Laurence Laughlin, William A. Scott, Horace White,
and H. Parker Willis—all of whom believed that the nation's money
stock would take care of itself if issued against commercial paper
arising from real transactions (Mints 1945: 206–7n33; West 1977:
chap. 7). The doctrine was attacked in 1905 by A. Piatt Andrew, who
spotlighted the two-way inflationary interaction between money and
prices inherent in the real bills mechanism. Of this inflationary feedback loop running from money to prices and back to money, Andrew
(1905: 111) wrote:

> Every new extension of credit [namely, bank loans supplied to
> borrowers in the form of newly created deposits], though based
> upon the money value of goods, would tend to raise the price
> level, and each elevation of the price level in its turn would justify
> a further extension of credit. The two movements might continue
> pursuing each other until eternity and yet the aggregate value
> of the means of payment [checking deposits] would not become
> co-extensive with the money value of all property. The alleged
> limitation of bank credit [and the money supply] by "the value of
> goods and property owned by borrowers" is from every point of
> view delusive. It is not only untrue; it is impossible.

Andrew saw that the Real Bills Doctrine embodies an inflationary transmission mechanism running from loans to money to prices to
the level of economic activity or needs of trade (a nominal magnitude

[11] A fourth mechanism to prevent overissue in a competitive, laissez-faire banking system was put
forth by the Free Banking School—namely, adverse interbank clearings (Arnon 2011: 264; White
1997: 47) Any bank that overissued relative to its competitors would find the superfluous notes returned to it through the clearinghouse for redemption in specie. Fear of such adverse clearings and the
resulting loss of gold reserves would discipline banks to refrain from excess issue, thus preserving price
stability. The rival Currency School, however, pointed out that this mechanism would fail to operate if
all banks overissued in concert. In that case, there would be no adverse interbank clearing balances to
prevent overissue.

that rises in step with prices) and back again to loans and money in a never-ending, explosive sequence. In short, because it cannot distinguish between the price and output components of economic activity, the real bills criterion, by itself, constitutes no bar to the inflationary overissue of money.

GERMAN HYPERINFLATION

By the late 19th and early 20th centuries, English Banking School ideas, while losing ground to rival Currency School ideas in England, had gained popularity in German monetary and banking circles. Accordingly, the Real Bills Doctrine formed the basis of the Reichsbank's policy of issuing astronomical sums of money to satisfy the needs of trade at ever-rising prices during the German hyperinflation of 1922–1923. Oblivious to Henry Thornton's 1802 demonstration that the real bills criterion is no bar to inflationary overissue when the borrowing rate is pegged below the going profit rate, the Reichsbank insisted on pegging its rediscount rate at 12 percent (later raised to 90 percent) at a time when the inflation-enhanced going market rate of interest was in excess of 7,000 percent per annum.[12] This huge rate differential, of course, made it extremely profitable for commercial banks to rediscount bills with the Reichsbank and to loan out the proceeds, thereby producing additional inflationary expansions of the money supply and further upward pressure on interest rates.

The Reichsbank's directors failed to perceive this inflationary process and did nothing to stop it. On the contrary, throughout the hyperinflation episode, the Reichsbank's president, Rudolf Havenstein, announced that he considered it his duty to supply the growing sums of money required to conduct real transactions at the skyrocketing prices, rises he attributed not to monetary overissue but to Germany's postwar reparations burden and other real shocks to the nation's external accounts. These shocks supposedly produced a causal chain running from reparations to balance-of-payments deficits to exchange rate

---

[12] This is the famous "Fisher Effect": The nominal market rate of interest tends to equal the real or price-deflated rate plus the expected rate of inflation, which at the height of the hyperinflation exceeded 7,000 percent per year.

depreciation to rising import prices and thence to rising general prices. Real shocks, not monetary ones, were allegedly to blame.

Appealing to the Real Bills Doctrine, Havenstein denied that issuing money to businessmen against the security of genuine commercial bills could have an inflationary impact. He simply failed to understand that linking the money supply to a nominal variable that moves in step with prices is tantamount to creating an engine of inflation. That is, he succumbed to the fallacy of using one uncontrolled nominal variable (the money value of real activity) to regulate another nominal variable (the money stock). Havenstein died of a heart attack just as the German monetary system disintegrated into a semi barter system when the hyperinflation played out in late 1923.

Not only did proponents of the Real Bills Doctrine, such as Havenstein and other Reichsbank officials and apologists, exonerate monetary expansion from causing inflation, they went to the opposite extreme as well (Humphrey 1980: 3–7). They treated such expansion not as a problem, but rather as the solution to an acute "shortage of money" caused by exogenously rising prices. As proof of the "monetary shortage," they cited the observed sharp drop in the real or price-deflated value of the money stock, which was far smaller than it had been before the inflation started.[13] They failed to realize that excessive nominal money growth itself was responsible for the shrinkage in the value of the real money stock. They did not see that explosive (and accelerating) rates of monetary growth were generating expectations of even faster future inflation. These inflationary expectations spurred a flight from cash—people wanted to spend the cash before it lost further purchasing power—and a corresponding rise in velocity. The rise in velocity caused prices to rise faster than the nominal money stock, thus producing the observed shrinkage in the real money stock.

This sequence of events, however, was beyond the Reichsbank director's comprehension. Hence, even though the nominal money stock was several trillion times larger than at the inflation's start,

---

[13] The chart reproduced by Humphrey (1980: 4) shows the German real money stock falling from a peak value of unity in May 1921 to a low of close to zero in October 1923. It originally appeared in Graham (1930: 105–6).

Havenstein and his colleagues argued that it still was not large enough to accommodate business at the higher prices. They thought they could prevent further collapse of the real money stock, and even restore it to its preinflation level, through additional massive increases in the nominal stock. They could not understand that efforts to arrest and reverse declines in the real money stock via faster nominal monetary growth would only serve to intensify and prolong those declines.

THE REAL BILLS DOCTRINE AS A METASTABLE MECHANISM

The preceding points have implicated the Real Bills Doctrine in Germany's unstable hyperinflationary monetary regime of 1923. The doctrine by itself, however, does not imply either a stable or an unstable system. That is why it is sometimes labeled "metastable" or "beyond" stable. The condition for stability lies "beyond" the doctrine itself; it depends completely on the institutional environment in which the doctrine appears. If, as in the German regime, the environment is inflationary due to a monetary authority that has a "rationale" for issuing money, the Real Bills Doctrine becomes part of that inflationary policy. It has no built-in quality to counter or reverse any ongoing inflationary policies. Likewise, if, as in the Great Depression of the early 1930s, some kind of political decisionmaking destroys money—say, by adverse actions against banks that create money—prices will fall until the outside influence that is provoking the deflation is arrested. In neither case does the doctrine itself initiate the instability that appears. It only becomes a part of the problem. The instability is in the financial environment. The Real Bills Doctrine itself does not cause the problem, but neither is it a force for stopping it.

Economist Lance Girton (1974) devised a simple money supply and demand diagram to illustrate how the political-economic environment operating through the doctrine can produce ever rising or falling prices. Girton presented only the stable-equilibrium version of the diagram in which the money demand curve cuts the money supply curve from below. Our version (Figure 2), the mirror image of his, shows the unstable-equilibrium case in which demand cuts supply from above. While Girton does not treat our case, it is clear from his discussion that the institutional framework in which the doctrine operates determines which case is relevant. If gold convertibility or some other effective constraint operates, it will discipline the doctrine to provide stability. But if no such constraint is functioning, the doctrine provides at best a metastable equilibrium—that is, an equilibrium only as stable as the political-economic system itself, which in the German hyperinflation was inherently unstable.

FIGURE 2

Money Supply and Demand

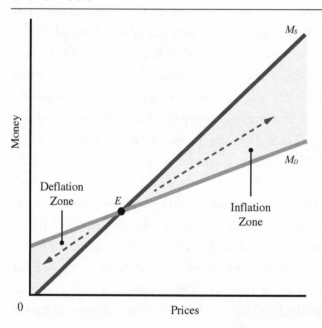

Figure 2 measures the money stock along the vertical axis and the general price level along the horizontal axis. With real output assumed constant, the diagram plots money supply and demand schedules as increasing linear functions of the price level. Money supply (M_s) rises with prices because rising prices boost the nominal needs-of-trade value of real activity, thereby justifying, via the Real Bills Doctrine, further increases in the money stock. Likewise, money demand (M_D)

rises with prices because people need to hold more cash to buy the unchanged real output at rising prices. However, the money demand schedule does not rise as steeply as the money supply schedule, so the demand curve cuts the supply curve from above at equilibrium point E.

This equilibrium is unstable, with disturbances to it causing ever-larger deviations from equilibrium, as shown by the arrows pointing away from E. In the inflation zone to the right of point E, money supply lies everywhere above money demand. This excess of money supply over demand produces ever-rising prices as people attempt to rid themselves of the unwanted excess money by spending it away on the fixed output. Conversely, in the deflation zone to the left of E, money demand lies everywhere above money supply. This excess demand for money produces ever-falling prices as people attempt to restore their cash balances to the desired level by spending less. Throughout, the money demand curve is less responsive to price changes than the money supply curve, which responds one-for-one as shown by its 45-degree slope. Money demand is less sensitive to prices because of the counteracting influence of price expectations. In the inflation zone, people expect prices to be higher, and thus the purchasing power of money lower, in the future. They expect as much because of the actions and statements of policymakers, both of which signal likely higher future inflation. The anticipated depreciation cost of holding money causes people to demand less of it than they otherwise would, so the money demand schedule lies below the money supply schedule. Conversely, in the deflation zone to the left of E, people expect future prices to be lower, and money's purchasing power higher, than currently. The anticipated appreciation return, or yield, on money holding induces people to demand more cash balances than they otherwise would, resulting in the money demand curve lying above the money supply curve.

In the German situation, a series of shocks, real and nominal, disturbed equilibrium and pushed the economy into the inflationary zone. Hyperinflation ensued. Conversely, in the 1930s Great Depression, economic disturbances and policy errors forced the economy into the deflationary zone. Falling prices (and output) followed.

VESTIGIAL REMAINS OF THE DOCTRINE

Our intellectual history would be remiss if it failed to say a word about the doctrine's current status. As noted in subsequent chapters, the doctrine's use as a policy guide faded away in the mid-to-late 1930s. Nevertheless, certain remnants, residues, and remains of the doctrine survive to this day. They include the fallacy that one uncontrolled nominal (dollar) variable can be used to control or regulate another. In the case of the Real Bills Doctrine, of course, the nominal variables consisted of the dollar value of production and the money stock. Today the same fallacy persists in the notion that the Fed should set the nominal interest rate "low" so as to spur spending, letting the money supply be as large as necessary to support that rate.[14] Both versions of the fallacy establish a potential for unlimited inflationary money growth.[15]

A second surviving remnant is the doctrine's anti-speculation animus. It persists currently in demands that the Fed prevent asset price bubbles and pop them when they occur. Both versions of the animus assume, without warrant, that the Fed can unerringly recognize speculation and distinguish it from production.

---

[14] See Sargent (1979: 92), who refers to the claim "that the proper function of the monetary authorities is to set the interest rate at some reasonable [i.e., 'low'] level, allowing the money supply to be whatever it must be to ensure that the demand for money at that rate is satisfied." This argument, Sargent notes, is akin to "the real bills rule" according to which "the quantity of money would automatically be properly regulated if the monetary authorities ensured that banks always had enough reserves to meet the demand for loans intended to finance 'real' (as opposed to 'speculative') investments at an interest rate set 'with a view to accommodating commerce and business.'" See also Girton (1974: 56), who states that low-interest-rate and cheap-money policies are "a close substitute for a real-bills money supply mechanism, and subject to the same defect."

[15] The idea here is that the low interest rate determines the amount of money the public wants to hold at that rate with the quantity of money supplied adapting passively to that demand. Money is demand determined with causation running from spending to interest rate to quantity of money demanded to quantity supplied. Trouble arises if the pegged low rate is below the level the market wants it to be. Then the money stock must be ever increasing to sustain the low pegged rate.

REAL BILLS IN THE COMMERCIAL BANK CLEARINGHOUSE SYSTEM

Bankers who initiated banking enterprises in the United States were no less believers in the Real Bills Doctrine as the guiding principle in managing a bank than were their English and other European forbears. Real bills or not, however, the commercial banking system that evolved in the United States during the 19th century was not accepted enthusiastically, or even graciously, by the general public and their political representatives. Bankers made money. Indeed, they made too much money, as far as many people were concerned. Reflecting this populist sentiment, laws—both state and federal—governing the commercial banking system in the United States between 1865 and 1900 altered the banking structure in the following ways:

- "Unit" banks (i.e., banks without any branches; all capital and lending operations were in a single location) proliferated. They were much too small to be efficient and, therefore, were not very profitable. By 1900 the United States had more than 12,000 unit banks.

- Banks were not allowed to branch either from state to state or within a state, or even in most of the cities where they were located, thus preventing them from realizing economies of scale or accruing defensive reserves in case of sudden demands on the reserves of one branch.

- Banks at every level faced legal reserve requirements that locked up their reserves and hindered them from adjusting most economically to the variable demands for hand-to-hand currency that occurred from time to time.

- Banking laws prevented banks from employing other lines of defense, such as the right to issue "due bills" and "post notes" at interest.[1]

The federal government, after the Civil War and with the gold standard in remission, had come to monopolize the issues of all currency—gold, silver, U.S. notes (greenbacks), silver certificates, and national banknotes.[2] All these currencies were both high-powered money—bank reserves—and, to a greater or lesser degree, hand-to-hand currency. Consequently, when people tried to cash in demand deposits for currency for whatever purpose, they depleted bank reserves, and with them the demand deposits that constituted the bulk of the money stock. Had the banks had control over their own defenses, such as the power to form branches, to adjust their reserve ratios on the basis of their business needs, or to issue post notes and due bills, nothing significant would have happened when a liquidity crisis threatened. But with these adjustment mechanisms denied them by contrary laws, an increased demand for hand-to-hand currency often resulted in reserve withdrawals and reduced loans and discounts, sometimes to such an extent that the total supply of demand deposits declined. Here, then, is an example of perverse elasticity: an increase in demand for money resulted in a decrease in supply! No commodity or service produced in a free market system ever suffered from this problem.[3]

Instead, the U.S. banking system, with the vulnerabilities noted, suffered periodic crises. Because of their built-in—that is, *legislated*—weaknesses, banks would occasionally suspend specie and legal tender

---

[1] See McCulloch (1986: 79–85) and Dowd (1995: 1–30). A fractional reserve commercial bank that faced more demands for cash than its cash reserves could pay would offer to pay its creditors interest for some short time period if they would agree to defer their demands for cash until the specified date. That was a "due bill." A "post note" was a currency item that promised the bearer redemption plus interest at some future (early) date. The two means of redemption were thus very similar. Both allowed the bank *time* to acquire the additional means for redemption that it needed.

[2] State banknotes, which had been the primary form of hand-to-hand currency, were prohibited by law in 1866. Consequently, the many banks that did not want to become "national" developed demand deposits as their "credit" means for discounting real bills.

[3] This perverse result of an increased demand for currency resulting in a *decreased* supply of total money appeared in the U.S. banking system in 1933 (see Chapter 8).

U.S. note (greenback) redemptions of demand deposits. Such "panics" appeared in 1873, 1893, and 1907.[4]

Bankers, being as self-sufficient as any other businessmen, realized that they had to build defenses against sudden and unforeseen demands on their banks for redemptions in specie or whatever was held as reserves. They also understood that their holdings of real bills would not serve as acceptable redemption media for their outstanding demand obligations. The real bills were redeemable in 30, 60, or 90 days, but the demand for redemption of outstanding notes or deposits was right now.

Fortunately, routine bank management included a payments mechanism—the clearinghouse system—which provided banks with a means for treating unusual demands for redemption. Banks originally had to clear checks and banknote currency issued by other banks by sending such items back to their issuing banks for payment in specie. This clearing operation was costly and cumbersome. To reduce these costs, banks in New York City established a central clearing bank where representatives from all the other banks in the city would meet, present their claims to each other, and strike a balance that would be cleared by immediate payments from deficit banks to creditor banks. Banks in other cities and large towns also adopted this practice. Commonly, every bank would leave some reserves in the clearinghouse to pay for unusual amounts of day-to-day debits against its reserves, and the clearinghouse management would issue certificates to the bank for those deposits of specie and other legal tender.[5]

Beginning in 1857, the New York clearinghouse used the clearinghouse balances of the commercial banks within its district as a reserve base to advance short-term loans in the form of clearinghouse loan certificates to some banks that were temporarily reserve-deficient. By this action, the New York clearinghouse became a fractional reserve institution and at the same time a lender of last resort to reserve-deficient banks within its province.

---

[4] For an account of these panics, see Friedman and Schwartz (1963: 89–168) and Timberlake (1993: 84–198).

[5] For a detailed account of the appearance of the clearinghouse association as a lender-of-last-resort in alleviating panics, see Timberlake (1993: 198–213).

Over the next 50 years, clearinghouses appeared in all the major cities and gradually in many smaller cities as well. So, too, did banking crises because of the restrictive banking laws, noted above, that both burdened the banks and hampered their defenses. In the presence of these laws, banks around the country built on the clearinghouse credit system that the New York clearinghouse had initiated. With the holdings of clearinghouse certificates, which had become assets of the participating banks, clearinghouse loan committees began to make loans in the form of clearinghouse loan certificates to needy banks that presented the right kind of short-term, self-liquidating paper—that is, *real bills*—for discount.

At first, the new currency—the clearinghouse loan certificates—was in large denomination bills in the $5,000–$10,000 range, which meant they were suitable only for bank clearings. Each succeeding bank panic, however, led to an extension of the clearinghouse system. More clearinghouses appeared. They made more loans on the basis of clearinghouse loan certificates; and the denominations of notes became smaller and smaller until many of the notes could be used as hand-to-hand currency and not just as supplemental bank reserves.

Because the laws passed in 1862 and 1864 prohibited issues of private money, the lending operations of clearinghouses had to be discreet. Bankers had to deny that the clearinghouse loan certificate issues were "money." They did so, and courts of law confirmed their claim. This indulgence reflected the fact that the system worked so well and prevented so much distress that to prohibit the issues of such notes or to fine their issuers would have provoked many disagreeable social problems. As A. Barton Hepburn (1924: 352) wrote in reviewing the 1893 panic, "This temporary currency . . . performed so valuable a service . . . that the government, after due deliberation, wisely forbore to prosecute. It is worthy of note that no loss resulted from the use of this make-shift currency." It worked so well that no clearinghouse loans ever resulted in any losses (Timberlake 1993: 203).

Another very reputable economist, A. Piatt Andrew, charged that the clearinghouse currency issued in 1907 "was an inconvertible [into gold] paper money issued without the sanction of law . . . yet necessitated by conditions for which our banking laws did not provide. . . . [It] doubtless prevented multitudes of bankruptcies which otherwise would have occurred" (Andrew 1908: 496–502). Indeed, the banking laws did not provide solutions. They were the problem, the principal one being reserve requirement laws that substituted rigid ratios for the judgments of bankers.

The success of the clearinghouse system raises the question of why it was abandoned. Why was a government central bank superimposed on a private system that had worked so well? Here was a real bills institution, still operating within the discipline of the gold standard, providing abundant private banking defenses for the system's weaknesses. Why not keep it?

The answers to this question reflect the mindsets of many contemporary observers and policymakers. First, the clearinghouse issues were so functional and at the same time so recognizably illegal that they had a hucksterish quality. Never mind that current banking laws restricted banks from providing their own defenses, the consensus was that "the government" should become the lender of last resort so that the extensions of bank credit would be "legitimate."

Second, the clearinghouse currency was market regulated; it was created and accepted voluntarily. When a panic had ended, the clearinghouse "central bank" disappeared. Its critics, however, would not recognize this feature. They insisted on an "official" government-issued currency, similar in form to national banknotes.

Third, the clearinghouse currency seemed to arise out of nothing. Few observers understood how a bank-related institution could create an emergency currency without seeming to have an emergency reserve base. It smacked of Wall Street legerdemain. Spontaneous market solutions seemed always to be greeted with skeptical mistrust.

Fourth, the clearinghouse issues were linked with the restriction and suspension of legitimate cash payments. Popular opinion presumed, incorrectly, that to some extent the clearinghouse actions caused the suspensions—an example of correlation implying causation.

Almost without exception, the official consensus was that some kind of central banking institution was the logical and sophisticated answer to the clearinghouse system. What reformers did not recognize was that a government-operated system would introduce a discretionary political element into monetary decisionmaking and thereby divorce the authority for making such decisions from those who had a self-interest in maintaining the system's integrity.

4

THE REAL BILLS EMPHASIS IN
THE FEDERAL RESERVE ACT

Congress's design for the Federal Reserve System reflects the significant real bills thinking and institutional promotion over the period 1908–1912, when the bills that would ultimately result in the Federal Reserve Act of 1913 were introduced. Most of that thinking favored the gold standard and was highly critical of Treasury interventions in financial markets. Many critics were economists solidly in support of the Real Bills Doctrine. One of them, J. Laurence Laughlin, was a University of Chicago economist and actively engaged with the American Bankers Association. Another, H. Parker Willis, a former student of Laughlin and professor of economics at Columbia University, became the special adviser to the chairman of the House Banking and Currency Committee, Rep. (later Sen.) Carter Glass of Virginia.[1] Willis was the principal economist helping Glass write the Federal Reserve Act. In fact, a substantial proportion of the profession had a real bills tendency.

In one effort to address the problems of the currency system as the Panic of 1907 played out, E. R. A. Seligman, a professor of political economy at Columbia University, organized a series of weekly lectures "to contribute to the understanding of the panic of 1907, and to lay down some principles which might be of service in the reconstruction of the currency system." Those lectures were published in 1908 (Seligman 1908).

The lecturers Seligman selected were prominent bankers or financiers and not necessarily economists. One of them was A. Barton Hepburn, a prominent banker and banking historian cited earlier, whose lecture was titled, "Government Currency vs. Bank Currency."

[1] See Bornemann (1940), Friedman and Schwartz (1963: 189–96), and Hepburn (1924: 397–410).

In his lecture, Hepburn reviewed the history of money and banking in the United States. He concluded by observing, "Judged from an historical and scientific standpoint, the currency system of a country can best be administered through the instrumentality of a central bank of issue." Hepburn's central bank would be similar in design to the central banks in Europe. It would earn a modest return on its capital, "but at the same time," he claimed, "the altruistic influences, personated [sic] by the government would largely control." He concluded with a rhetorical question: "Why will not a government-controlled central bank of issue, where the banks of the country in good credit can . . . discount their receivables, receiving the proceeds thereof in banknotes, afford the best solution to the currency question?"[2] From a present-day perspective, such a rhetorical question may seem naive. However, at that time the federal government still faced real constitutional constraints, especially those imposed by the gold standard.

The next lecturer, Albert Strauss, also a prominent banker, noted that the banking system lacked elasticity—that is, the supply of currency that the banks held as reserves could not adjust to accommodate the demand for hand-to-hand currency in market transactions without severely reducing bank-created deposits by a *multiple* of the currency withdrawn. Strauss's criticism was a common observance of the time. To provide this flexibility, Strauss favored a central bank. He believed that "a form of organization can be devised that will effectually protect it from the danger of political control or influence" (Seligman 1908: 85–86).

Paul Warburg, another prominent banker of the day who had many European connections, gave the lecture "American and European Banking Methods and Bank Legislation." Warburg argued that an "ideal banking system" would "provide for the maximum use of credit and the minimum use of cash [reserves]" and would be able to avoid all "violent convulsions." He thought European central banks managed their systems wisely, while the U.S. banking system was "wrong from top to bottom." He also emphasized the extensive branching

[2] Quoted in Seligman (1908: 59).

capabilities of European banks but, unfortunately, did not discuss the lack thereof in the American system (Seligman 1908: 132).

Warburg noted, too, the incongruity between the bounteous reserves that American banks possessed and their reluctance to use them. "While one thousand millions of dollars were lying idle in our banks and trust companies as so-called reserves," he noted, "this money, by virtue of the law could scarcely be touched." After making this accurate criticism, however, he offered no suggestions as to how that problem might be remedied and the reserves used, except that all banks' reserves should be kept by the central bank (Seligman 1908: 138). Warburg also approved of "a central clearing house, with power to issue [notes] against clearinghouse certificates," which would be guaranteed by the government. However, this solution, he argued, should be only temporary. In his view, the clearinghouse system was a less-than-optimal surrogate for a central bank (Seligman 1908: 138).

These financial lecturers were largely concerned with developing some kind of super-banking institution that would provide "form-seasonal elasticity" to the monetary system to prevent the kind of banking crisis that had just occurred.[3] None of them favored continuing the clearinghouse system. Nor did they seem to realize that the banks, despite all their other restrictions, had plenty of reserves to avert a suspension—but the use of those reserves was immobilized by legal reserve requirements. Consequently, the discussion favored a new institution that, in J. Laurence Laughlin's words, would be "wholly free from politics or outside influence—as much respected for character and integrity as the Supreme Court—which shall be able to use government bonds or selected securities, as a basis for the issue of forms of lawful money, which could be added to the reserves of the banks." However, Laughlin added, "It is doubtful if a great central bank—apart from its political impossibility—would accomplish the desired end" (Laughlin 1907: 609).

---

[3] A monetary system has "form-seasonal elasticity" when one form of money—say, currency—can be converted into another form—say, bank demand deposits (checkbook balances)—without undue change in the total quantity of money.

Laughlin was clearly anti–central bank. He was a real bills con-servative who had no use for a central bank of the European design. Yet, just what kind of supplemental banking institution *would* satisfy the various norms of the critics and come into financial markets at just the right time was not at all clear. Everyone knew that some kind of "credit" had to be created to furnish banks the reserves they lacked, and it had to be an open market purchase by a government agency. Whereas Laughlin would have allowed some amount of government securities to be the open market vehicle, most economists, bankers, legislators, and pundits favored a currency based on private loans and discounts—that is, the real bills of commercial banks.

Congress duly discussed various proposals and passed the makeshift Aldrich-Vreeland Act in 1908. This act grouped national banks—that is, banks chartered by the Comptroller of the Currency and the Secretary of the Treasury—into 10-bank clusters that would mimic the private clearinghouses. Their powers would include clear-ing checks as well as issuing notes on the basis of commercial paper "under the direction and control of the Secretary of the Treasury." The notes would be taxed at the rate of 5 percent for the first month and 1 percent additional each month thereafter in order to limit their issue and duration.[4]

The Aldrich-Vreeland Act also provided for the creation of a National Monetary Commission to examine banking and central banking systems in the United States and Europe. The commission had authority to farm out research grants for this purpose. After some years, during which the researchers did their investigations, many of which were published as books, Sen. Nelson W. Aldrich (R-NY) commented on their content in an address to the Economic Club of New York.

The new organization, Aldrich noted, should not copy the cen-tral banking institutions of other countries "without many material modifications." It should, however, have a monopoly over the issue of currency. It would mobilize and centralize reserves and control its

---

[4] *Congressional Record*, 60th Cong., 1st sess., 6323 and 6375 (1908). The Secretary of the Treasury was never left out of *any* proposed central banking plan.

lending operations by means of a discount rate. Its gold reserve should be "used" to the extent necessary (Aldrich 1910).[5]

In accordance with the commission's recommendations, Congress considered a bill to create a National Reserve Association, which President William Howard Taft supported. Such an association would eliminate, Taft said, "the troublesome question" of a central bank.[6]

But would it? A representative from Alabama, Richard Hobson, cited a "critical analysis by a Mr. R. C. Milliken, a 'monetary expert' in the securities business." Milliken argued that the National Reserve Association would be no different from a European central bank. He also noted that it would impose reserve requirements, an idea with which he found much fault. He then offered a principle for the institution's discounting operations: the institution should discount only bills "issued for productive credit arising from real commercial transactions to solvent persons furnishing convertible paper payable at short and fixed periods."[7] No one ever penned a more accurate description of real bills.

However, the National Reserve Association—real bills or not, central bank or not—was not to be. The political structure of the federal government began to change in 1910, and the elections of 1910 and 1912 brought in both a Democratic president and a Democratic Congress. With Democrats in control of both houses of Congress and the presidency, the budding monetary institution had to be changed and its sponsors had to be Democrats. This mutation took place in the next (63rd) Congress.

Rep. Carter Glass, a Democrat from Virginia, became chairman of the House Committee on Banking and Currency after the 1912 elections and introduced a bill to create a Federal Reserve System in the summer of 1913. In his bill, Glass cited major deficiencies of the existing system: First, no reserve was available to the banking system

[5] By including the word "used," Aldrich was implying a control over the gold standard that was neither warranted nor constitutional. His defection from a gold standard that operated as the Constitution implied was both telling and prophetic. For an excellent analysis of the Aldrich episode, see Selgin (2017: 123–74).

[6] *Congressional Record*, 62nd Cong., 2nd sess., 587 (1911).

[7] *Congressional Record*, 62nd Cong., 2nd sess., 484–87 (1911).

at critical times.[8] Second, all the currency in circulation, primarily national banknotes, but also silver certificates and the fixed stock of greenbacks, was based on "the Nation's debt," that is, on outstanding government securities, rather than on something that would reflect the variable needs of business, such as the short-term paper—real bills—of commercial banks.[9]

It may seem strange in retrospect, but any institution that looked like a central bank was politically impossible with congressional Democrat majorities. This sentiment reflected the "sound money" principles of the Jacksonian Democrats in the 1830s. In lieu of such an undesirable institution, the House Banking and Currency Committee proposed a Federal Reserve System of 8 to 12 independent regional reserve banks. The proper number was suggested by Sen. John Shafroth of Colorado when the bill got to the Senate.

The president of a bank in need of accommodation, Shafroth noted, "should be able to pack up enough 30-, 60-, and 90-day commercial paper he wanted cashed, take the train for the city where the Federal Reserve bank is situate, and be able to wire [back] that he had cashed sufficient securities to meet the demand of all depositors." Shafroth contrasted this model with "one central bank located several days' run from many of the interior banks." A regional system, he argued, would also preserve the personal relationship between the commercial banker and his regional Reserve bank colleague.[10] Shafroth's scenario of a bank in need and a Federal Reserve super-bank standing by to fulfill that need expressed very well the reserve-in-emergency nature of what many legislators were seeking.

During the debates, much discussion focused on who would control the reserve banks. One argument was that the "people" should control the banks. But who are "the people?" asked one senator, to which Sen. Alben Barkley of Kentucky replied, "The Government is

---

[8] It is indeed incredible that public figures, such as Glass and many others including academics, could make this claim. The banks had all kinds of reserves that were simply unavailable because of federal laws specifying banks' reserve requirements.

[9] *Congressional Record*, 63rd Cong., 1st sess., 4642–44 (1912).

[10] *Congressional Record*, 63rd Cong., 1st sess., 6021 (1912).

the people, and the people act through their authorized agents, the chief of whom is the President of the United States."[11]

Representative Glass, however, was eager to promote the non-political nature of the new system, even though others denied that this feature was possible. Sen. James Lewis of Illinois stated: "The bill is political, political to the extent that it voices the political ideas of the people of this country, political in that it expresses in legislation the platform of the [Democratic Party]. . . . All things must be guided, honorable sir. To some men each system must be intrusted [sic]."[12]

The debates on the bill offered different norms for control of banks and money and corresponding conclusions about the proper agency for control, depending on whether the observer was speaking about the proposed Federal Reserve Board of Governors, the Federal Reserve banks, or the monetary system in general. In addition to these possible controlling bodies was the question of what devices the different institutions should use to control whatever was to be controlled. With all these variables, the debates became at times both confused and confusing.

One principle, however, was paramount: whatever the agency in charge, the essential medium for policy would be real bills. "The only limit to a commercial bank's ability to discount," said Rep. Charles Korbly of Indiana, "is the limit to good commercial paper. . . . Such paper springs from self-clearing transactions." When a banker knew the rediscounting privilege would be refused on noneligible paper, he would be anxious to confine his loans accordingly. "The whole purpose of the Federal Reserve Act," Korbly emphasized, "is to enforce this practice."[13]

Since "eligible" meant "real bills" and since such paper was naturally limited, some congressmen wanted to make rediscounting a right rather than a privilege granted by the authority of either a board or a bank. Again, only short-term paper generated by the production of

---

[11] *Congressional Record,* 63rd Cong., 1st sess., 4790 (1912). Barkley later became vice president of the United States in the administration of President Harry Truman, 1948–1952.

[12] *Congressional Record,* 63rd Cong., 1st sess., 1480–81 (1912).

[13] *Congressional Record,* 63rd Cong., 1st sess., 4661–63 (1912).

real goods and services was eligible. "Short-time commercial paper, which is liquid and collects itself [provides] a natural system of elasticity," concluded Sen. Knute Nelson of Minnesota.[14]

Another view of the Fed banks was that they should act as a "public utility" similar to the Interstate Commerce Commission. The new Fed, some congressmen suggested, should "give the borrowing public a stable and uniform low rate of interest" in the same way that the Interstate Commerce Commission established low freight rates.[15] This idea, however, was dismissed without much argument.

Somewhat akin to the public utility image of the new Fed was the view that the new Fed Board would act as a "supreme court of finance." However, Rep. L. C. Dyer of Missouri properly disputed this view, noting that Supreme Court justices were appointed for life and were trained specifically for legal practice, whereas the proposed Fed act actually prohibited any officer or stockholder of a banking institution from being appointed to the Fed Board due to a possible conflict of interest.[16]

At least one senator, Elihu Root of New York, observed that the new Fed Board would face "no limit whatever on the quantity of notes that may be issued" and that the reserve banks were similarly unconstrained in their discounting procedures. Root did not agree that real bills were an effective check in themselves to commercial bank lending. He warned against loans made "upon security that is good until the time comes when, through a process of inflation, we reach a situation in which no security is good." Then "the standards which are applied in the exercise of that kind of judgment [for real bills discounting] become modified by the optimism of the hour and grow less and less effective in checking the expansion of business."[17]

Root's complaint exposed the instability that a real bills policy may aggravate—an instability that a dominant gold standard prevented. While he discussed only the inflationary instability, the same

---

[14] *Congressional Record*, 63rd Cong., 2nd sess., 523 (1912).

[15] *Congressional Record*, 63rd Cong., 1st sess., 6016 (1913).

[16] *Congressional Record*, 63rd Cong., 1st sess., 4680 (1913).

[17] *Congressional Record*, 63rd Cong., 1st sess., 966–67 (1913).

argument holds for a downturn and its development into a depression. Root, however, did not discuss the necessity for a dominant gold standard to prevent real bills excesses, nor did any other senator or representative.

Sen. Robert Owen of Oklahoma, one of the Democratic sponsors of the legislation, claimed that the Reserve Board could set the discount rate at any level that would discourage borrowing. Sen. John Williams of Mississippi supported Owen's arguments. The Fed Board, he claimed, has "no power to initiate, to compel or to consummate any inflation whatsoever. [It has] a power to compel contraction . . . either by raising the interest rate or by refusing its approval to the issue of paper currency by the reserve banks."[18] Sixteen years later—early 1929—Williams's explanation was to become a precise description of current Fed policy.

Up to this point, the role of the gold standard within a Federal Reserve banking system had been largely neglected. However, when the legislators had to discuss the new Fed banks' balance sheets, after the banks had issued Federal Reserve note currency or credited the reserve accounts of member banks, they came to realize that a gold standard was still the law of the land and vitally important to the payments system.

The Treasury at the time, through the Comptroller of the Currency, monitored three fiat currencies: U.S. notes (greenbacks), silver certificates, and national banknotes. Against the fixed quantity of $346.7 million U.S. notes, the Treasury kept by law a statutory gold reserve of $150 million, which implied a gold reserve ratio of 43.3 percent. Using these data, the consensus was to fix the gold reserve requirement against outstanding Federal Reserve notes at 40 percent. Other arguments resulted in a gold reserve ratio against member bank reserves of 35 percent. The bill also included a provision allowing the Fed banks to operate with deficient gold reserves against these moneys, requiring them to pay a graduated tax on any such deficiency.[19]

[18] *Congressional Record*, 63rd Cong., 1st sess., 903 (1913).

[19] *Congressional Record*, 63rd Cong., 1st sess., 1196 and 1358 (1913).

The debate over reserve requirements for the Fed banks revealed what everyone sensed—that eligible paper (i.e., real bills) would not necessarily limit excessive bank lending without also a gold reserve requirement. The gold standard was still the only certain constraint to money creation. Even so, Senator Owen could argue that Federal Reserve notes would not be a fiat currency because they "are secured by commercial bills of a highly qualified class."[20] The very fact that Fed notes—currency—had a higher required gold ratio than member bank reserves against bank deposits implied that congressmen did not understand how an increase in bank reserves—say, from gold deposits—would serve as a basis for the fractional reserve banking system to expand its deposits to a multiple of any increase in gold reserves.[21]

After many hundreds of pages of debate, when the bill neared a final vote in December 1913, Republican minority spokesmen against the bill, who had been in the House-Senate conference committee, complained that they had not received proper recognition of their arguments. But Senator Shafroth retorted that the Democratic majority had properly condemned the whole concept of a central bank, while every Republican member had supported it. Their views could not be tolerated, he exclaimed; the Democratic majority would never create a central bank![22]

Rather, the new Federal Reserve banks would be a special part of the commercial banking system and would operate as clearinghouses in their districts. Senator Owen confirmed that the new system had evolved from "the clearance-house [sic] associations. . . . This bill, for the most part," he argued, "is merely putting into legal shape that which hitherto has been illegally done"—that is, by the private clearinghouse system.[23] It is doubtful that Senator Owen knew anything fundamental about how the clearinghouse system had worked as a lender of last resort. Some political opponent who did should have asked him: If the clearinghouse lending system operated illegally, but had such beneficial effects, and without any losses from their issues of currency, why not

[20] *Congressional Record*, 63rd Cong., 1st sess., 979 (1913).

[21] See remarks by Sen. Albert Cummins of Iowa (*Congressional Record*, 63rd Cong., 1st sess., 466 (1912).

[22] *Congressional Record*, 63rd Cong., 1st sess., 1353–56 (1913).

[23] *Congressional Record*, 63rd Cong., 1st sess., 4652 (1913).

just change the laws so that they would be "legal"? Strangely enough, this alternative was never considered and, of course, was never debated.

One of the last provisions discussed in the House debate was an explicit reference to the gold standard. The final version read, "Nothing in this act . . . shall be considered to repeal the parity provisions contained in an act [the Currency ('Gold Standard') Act] approved March 14, 1900." Necessary or not, the reference was left in. The new Fed was not to serve as a surrogate for the traditional gold standard.[24]

Congress passed the Federal Reserve Act on December 23, 1913, but not before much dissent and some very close votes on various provisions. On final passage, Rep. Charles A. Lindbergh Sr. of Minnesota noted that the act "establishes the most gigantic trust on earth, such as the Sherman Antitrust Act would dissolve if Congress did not by this act expressly create what by that act it prohibited."[25] Most regrettably, the passage of the new act meant that the former private clearinghouse system, which had worked so well, was essentially eliminated as a lender of last resort.

The 1913 act gave the Fed Board significant statutory powers over the activities of the regional Fed banks. The Board had veto power over discount rates that the Fed banks set, as well as the power "to review and determine the character of the paper eligible for discount"—that is, the nature of the real bills that the Fed banks bought from needy banks to provide them with new reserves.[26] However, the Fed banks were the institutions that provided the loans and rediscounts to the member banks on their 30-, 60-, or 90-day paper. So, was the Fed Board supposed to decide, when reviewing the applications for lending, whether the Fed banks had made the proper decisions? How could the Board be privy to all the local necessities that the commercial banks and regional Fed banks had to deal with? And how then could a regional Fed bank provide loans and discounts in time for the loans' stated purposes? Indeed, the formal law, as written, was effectively inoperable.

---

[24] *Congressional Record*, 63rd Cong., 2nd sess., 5100–5106 (1913).

[25] *Congressional Record*, 63rd Cong., 2nd sess., 1446 (1913).

[26] It also had extensive emergency powers, as we discuss in Chapter 8.

$$\boxed{5}$$

THE REAL BILLS DOCTRINE AT
THE FED BOARD IN THE 1920s

While the Real Bills Doctrine encourages the use of short-term self-liquidating paper that promotes real product, it also has a dark side: It condemns three other kinds of debt that banks might promote. First, it calls for banks to shun loans that further any aspect of stock market activity—especially any kind of speculative lending in securities markets. Such lending, according to real bills proponents, is counterproductive because it does not lead to any kind of new production; it only churns up stock market prices. Second, the doctrine rejects real estate loans—mortgages—which may be productive in that they promote housing, but they violate the doctrine's short-term liability standard. Finally, the doctrine argues against purchases of government securities because such lending also violates the productivity criterion and encourages unproductive government deficits.

The Federal Reserve Act, signed into law in 1913, incorporated real bills principles into its text. It stated that "any Federal reserve bank may discount . . . notes, drafts, and bills of exchange issued or drawn for agricultural, industrial, or commercial purposes, or the proceeds of which have been used, or are to be used, for such purposes." It also included an equally important disclaimer: "Such definition shall not include notes, drafts, or bills covering merely investments issued or drawn for the purpose of carrying or trading in stocks, bonds, or other investment securities, except bonds and notes of the United States.[1] Notes, drafts, and bills admitted to discount under the terms of this paragraph must have a maturity at the time of discount of not more than 90 days" (Board of Governors 1961: 44).

---

[1] This exception permitting some government securities was put in as a political maneuver.

From the act's passage in 1913 until 1920, however, the new Fed was not to be the "bankers' bank" envisioned by its founders. Financing World War I put severe fiscal burdens on the U.S. Treasury. And since the secretary of the Treasury was also the chairman of the Federal Reserve Board, and the comptroller of the treasury was the vice-chairman, the new Federal Reserve System naturally became, *ipso facto*, a handmaiden for Treasury policies (Friedman and Schwartz 1963: 157; Timberlake 1993: 235).

This institutional arrangement promoted the postwar inflation of 1918–1920. The secretary of the Treasury pressured the Fed's Board of Governors, of which he was one and whose offices were conveniently placed in the Treasury building, to support the prices of government securities to keep market interest rates "low." By 1920, however, the regional Fed banks managed to shake themselves more or less free of the Treasury and the Fed Board in Washington and to begin operating in the mode roughly suggested by the Federal Reserve Act. They allowed their government debt holdings to run down, in accordance with Treasury debt-retirement policy; at the same time they allowed member bank reserve liabilities to decline. This correction caused the brief but sharp recession of 1920–1922. Only after 1922 were the Fed banks in a position to begin any truly independent operations (Friedman and Schwartz 1963: 231–40).

Even then, the 12 regional reserve banks had very little idea of how their operations should fit into the monetary-banking framework of the era. A gold standard was supposed to rule the monetary system. Fed banks were there simply to expedite the gold standard's adjustments and to serve as lenders of last resort to tide over solvent but illiquid banks during periods of disequilibrium in financial markets.

The Real Bills Doctrine had been bequeathed by 19th century Banking School economists to their Federal Reserve counterparts and was incorporated into the Federal Reserve Act of 1913 (see Appendix A for a formalized version of the Real Bills Doctrine).[2]

---

[2] Skaggs (2010, 477) disagrees. He contends that although the "creators and early leaders" of the Fed "had much to say in support of the real bills doctrine," the Banking School, by contrast, "had little to say about lending on real bills." Therefore, in Skaggs's words it is "simply wrong" to claim that the Fed inherited the doctrine from the Banking School. Our reading of both the Banking School and much of the interpretive scholarly literature on it convinces us, however, that the Banking School did indeed

Even so, the doctrine was hardly ready for official deployment. It needed to be equipped with empirical content before it could emerge in a form amenable to Fed use.

MAKING THE DOCTRINE OPERATIONAL

Fed Board economists in the early 1920s gave the doctrine operational content by defining its variables so that they could be measured and serve as policy guides. Output was defined as aggregate physical product as measured by the Board's monthly index of industrial production. Dating from December 1922 and constructed from data on output produced in manufacturing and mining, this index was principally the work of Walter Stewart and Woodlief Thomas. It had forerunners in the production indexes developed by Wesley Clair Mitchell for the War Production Board in 1917, by Carl Snyder for the New York Fed in 1918–1920, and by Stewart himself in 1921 before he left Amherst College to go to the Fed Board.

The Board gave this index pride of place in its collection of statistical indicators for two reasons. The index quantified the needs-of-business criterion of the Federal Reserve Act. It also represented the strategic real output variable that together with prices drove all other variables—loans, bills, money stock—in the real bills credit mechanism.

Likewise, the Board defined productive loans as bank credit advanced solely to finance the production and marketing of goods in the agricultural, industrial, and commercial sectors of the economy. (The Board also published in its monthly *Bulletin* figures on what it regarded as speculative lending, notably loans to brokers and dealers, real estate loans, and long-term capital investment loans.) The Board defined real bills as paper pledged as collateral for nonspeculative loans and eligible for rediscount at the Fed. The exact counterpart of productive loans, such bills constituted evidence of the Board's belief that the type of paper banks acquire in making loans, which finance real output, governs the particular use of the borrowed funds—real bills

---

adhere to the doctrine, which it bequeathed to the Fed's founding fathers. If so, one can trace a direct line of descent from the former group to the latter.

signify and measure productive credit just as non–real bills denote speculative credit.

This notion of strict correspondence between types of loan collateral and use of borrowed funds was not shared by all bankers and economists. As early as November 28, 1922, in a talk to the Graduate Economics Club at Harvard, Benjamin Strong of the New York Fed opposed the notion on the grounds that the fungibility of credit across uses renders the idea fallacious (Chandler 1958: 197–98). With credit interchangeable, banks and their customers could borrow on real bills to finance speculation. Conversely, they could borrow on speculative paper—stocks, bonds, and mortgages—to finance production. If so, then the type of paper is independent of the purpose of the loan, and there is no assurance that credit advanced on real bills will remain in productive channels. But many Fed officials—notably Adolph Miller and reserve bank governors John Calkins, James McDougal, George Norris, and George Seay—disagreed with Strong and throughout the 1920s continued to argue that the form of collateral denotes a particular use of borrowed funds.

The Board thought so little of the money stock as a strategic variable that it published no series of it before 1941. Nevertheless, the Board did collect data on the currency and demand deposit components of the money stock. It published extensive series on these individual components, including monthly figures on currency in circulation, a series on weekly reporting member banks that contained substantial detail on deposits, and a semiannual all-bank series that one could employ to establish benchmarks for monthly deposit estimates on the basis of deposits of reporting member banks. However, the Board never consolidated these components into a single comprehensive series on the money stock. Indeed, it had little reason to do so. Guided as it was by the Real Bills Doctrine, the Board saw money creation as simply a byproduct, or side effect, of bankers's lending decisions that financed real output. To the Board, loans, not money, were what mattered. Provided that banks made the right kind of loans, the money stock would take care of itself.

The final step in the Board's effort to make the doctrine operational involved defining the price level as measured by the wholesale price index. The Board attributed movements in this index either to the long-term operation of exogenous real forces, notably technological progress or resource scarcity, or to short-term speculation—that is, to "nonproductive" uses of money and credit. Secular price changes were ascribed either to cost-reducing productivity gains or to cost-raising resource limitations. Likewise, short-term increases in the price level were seen as evidence of a speculative withholding of goods from the market in anticipation of the higher future prices they might bring. And short-term declines in the price level were seen as the inevitable consequence of the bursting of the speculative bubble—as when goods were dumped on the market at fire-sale prices. The Board's inclination was to interfere little or not an all with these latter price falls. Indeed, it regarded them as necessary to purge the economy of its preceding speculative excesses. The upshot was that the Board watched the price index for evidence of speculation and its aftereffects rather than for evidence that money was easy or tight.

POLICY GUIDES IN THE BOARD'S 10TH ANNUAL REPORT

The Real Bills Doctrine figured prominently in the celebrated quantitative and qualitative policy guides featured in the Board's famous 1923 *Tenth Annual Report* (Board of Governors 1924), coauthored by Walter Stewart and Adolph Miller.[3] The guides, focusing as they did on stopping inventory speculation, were important anticipators of the Board's later eve-of-Depression crusade against stock market speculation in which member banks suspected of ever having made stock market loans were threatened with denial of Fed discount window assistance.

The *quantitative* guide held that money and credit should go to finance all real output except that intended for speculative inventory

[3] For critical evaluations of these guides, see Friedman and Schwartz (1963: 252–53) and Mints (1945: 265–68). For more sympathetic treatments, see Hardy (1932: 74–80), Reed (1930: 59–64), West (1977: 195–98), and Wicker (1966).

accumulation.[4] The danger was that such stockpiling would become excessive, leading to the dumping of surplus goods on markets at fire-sale prices to depress profits and real activity. The sharp postwar boom-bust cycle of 1919–1921 had taught Stewart and Miller that such outcomes were possible. It had revealed that credit expansion, by financing inventory overinvestment instead of production for final consumption, could lead to an inflationary shortage of consumer goods followed by deflation and recession when excess stocks of those goods finally flooded the market.

The *qualitative* guide held that real bills in bank portfolios constituted evidence that the quantitative test had been passed and that quantitative control could be achieved by qualitative means. After the mid-1920s, the Board abandoned quantitative guides in favor of qualitative ones when its concern shifted from accommodating production to stopping speculation in the stock market (see Reed 1930: 60, 63; Yohe 1990: 482). In this way a "marriage of the traditional real bills doctrine and an inventory theory of the business cycle," as Friedman and Schwartz put it, presaged Miller's 1929 crusade against stock market speculation (Friedman and Schwartz 1963: 252–53).

REJECTION OF THE QUANTITY THEORY IN STABILIZATION HEARINGS

The Fed Board's rejection of the quantity theory in the 1920s removed remaining doubts about its adherence to the Real Bills Doctrine. The Board opposed the activist intervention idea that control of money could stabilize prices. The passive-accommodation doctrine taught the Board that money is, or should be, output determined; that real forces drive prices; and that causation runs from prices (and real activity) to money rather than vice versa. Accordingly, when Congress held hearings in 1926–1927 and 1928 on Kansas Rep. James G. Strong's proposal to make price level stabilization an explicit goal of monetary

---

[4] For a classic account of the inventory proviso, see Hardy (1932: 77). The Fed's responsibility, he writes, is "not to check price increases [associated with expanding production and other real forces] but to supply a volume of credit appropriate to the higher prices, so long as the latter are not interpreted as evidence of speculative accumulation of inventories."

policy, the Board's real bills advocates testified to their opposition in no uncertain terms (see U.S. Congress 1927: 1929).[5]

They began with an attack on the general price level, or average of prices—the quantity theory's key variable. It was, they held, an unreliable indicator determined by forces—technical progress, productivity growth, resource scarcity, and so on—beyond the Fed's control. Other than preventing inventory speculation and resulting cyclical price movements, the Fed had no business interfering with price falls caused by cost-reducing technological progress or price rises due to exhaustion of scarce natural resource supplies. Missing was any recognition that monetary policy might be sufficiently powerful to counteract these real forces and keep general prices stable.

Missing also was the realization that if the Fed set the money stock equal to the demand for it so that total spending remained unchanged, the costs of production would affect the relative prices of individual goods but not the average price of all of them. When money supply equals money demand, cost-induced rises in the relative prices of some goods require consumers to spend more money on those goods. Less money is left to spend on other goods, whose prices accordingly fall. The rise in the first set of relative prices is offset by falls in the second set, leaving general prices unchanged. Advocates of the Real Bills Doctrine offered no rebuttal to this argument. Instead they disparaged the general price level on the grounds that people would confuse it with the prices of specific goods and assume that a policy of price level stabilization meant stabilization of the individual prices of those goods.

Proponents of the Real Bills Doctrine on the Fed Board also gave the money stock short shrift in their stabilization testimony, arguing that it was merely a by-product of bankers' loan decisions. Loans, not money, were what mattered. Provided that bankers made the right kind of loans, the money stock would take care of itself. In any case, the money stock could not be a means of deliberate policy because the Fed exercised no control over it. Businessmen determine the money

---

[5] On Fed testimony in the stabilization hearings, see Hetzel (1985), Hardy (1932: 207–18), and Meltzer (1997: 66–79).

stock through their demand for productive loans—or so the Board members contended.

Furthermore, they claimed, the money stock does not determine the price level. Rather, it adapts passively to the needs of trade at prevailing prices determined by the real forces of technological progress, productivity growth, and resource scarcity. Miller (U.S. Congress 1929: 109) said it all when he insisted that neither of the quantity theory's assumptions—namely, that the Fed causes changes in the money supply which in turn cause corresponding changes in the price level—is valid. He was referring to *secular* price changes, not *cyclical* price changes. He did associate *cyclical* price changes with money, albeit not with fluctuations in its quantity but rather with its inappropriate use to finance inventory speculation. As a result, he watched cyclical price indices for evidence of speculation and its aftermath rather than for information that money was plentiful or tight.

The upshot was that the Board's real bills advocates carried the day. Their contention that the quantity theory and its money stock and price level indicators were unfit for policy use convinced influential congressmen, economists, businessmen, and bankers alike. No price level target was enacted into law, and the Fed published no comprehensive money stock series until 1941.[6]

THE DOCTRINE AND OPEN MARKET OPERATIONS RECONCILED

The main interventionist challenge to the Real Bills Doctrine came from the Fed's discovery in 1922–1923 of open market operations as a means of reserve control. This discovery violated the doctrine's anti-interventionist precepts in at least three ways (see Chandler 1970). First, open market purchases and sales of U.S. government bonds conflict with the doctrine's contention that the Fed should deal solely in short-term, self-liquidating, private-sector commercial paper. Government bonds, according to the doctrine, represent nonproductive use of credit. Second, Fed open market operations are conducted at the initiative of the central

[6] Benjamin Strong of the New York Fed also rejected a price level target for Fed policy, but he did so because he anticipated the resumption of the gold standard. He recognized that policy had to be *either* a gold standard *or* a stable price level standard (see Burgess [1930] 1983: 317–31).

bank, not private business. Such active intervention clashes with the principle of passive accommodation, according to which the initiative for reserve provision should come not from the Fed but from member banks responding to the needs of trade. Third, open market operations contradict the doctrine's presumption that banks obtain all needed reserves at the discount window. There the Fed, according to the doctrine, passively accommodates all legitimate—that is, real bills–collateralized—demands for reserves sufficient to back the amount of money and credit that satisfy the needs of trade. With the discount window operating in this way, no other reserve source is necessary. As Wheelock (1991: 13) notes, "The Real Bills Doctrine implied that rediscounts alone would provide sufficient liquidity to accommodate commerce and meet financial emergencies. No [other sources of reserves] were necessary." How then could such a redundant and unnecessary instrument as open market operations be squared with the Real Bills Doctrine?

The Fed's "great discovery" of the famous scissors—or displacement—effect permitted the reconciliation (Burgess 1964: 220). It enabled proponents of the doctrine to interpret open market operations in a manner consistent with preservation of the doctrine.

Christened by Harold Reed, the scissors effect referred to the tendency of compensating changes in discount-window borrowing to offset open market operations, leaving total reserves unchanged (Reed 1930: 28).[7] W. Randolph Burgess and Benjamin Strong at the New York Fed, and Adolph Miller, Walter Stewart, and Winfield Riefler at the Fed Board, discovered this phenomenon in 1922–1923. To their surprise, they found that open market sales, by removing reserves, induced member banks to apply to the discount window to recoup the lost reserves. Conversely, Fed open market purchases, by increasing reserves, enabled member banks to pay off their indebtedness to the discount window. In both cases, compensatory changes in member bank borrowing at the discount window tended to counteract the reserve-expanding-and-contracting effects of open market operations. The result was that borrowed reserves varied inversely with open

---

[7] See also Friedman and Schwartz (1963: 251, 272, 296), Yohe (1990: 493), and U.S. Congress (1927: 749).

market operations, as measured by changes in the Fed's holdings of government securities, in a one-for-one, dollar-for-dollar relationship.[8]

The scissors effect prompted two interpretations of open market operations consistent with the Real Bills Doctrine. The first, advanced by Miller and Stewart, held that such operations constituted a test of whether reserves and the deposit money they supported were in excess of the needs of trade (Board of Governors 1924: 13–14). Open market operations were taken at the initiative of the Fed. But the initiative to borrow or repay at the discount window came from member banks seeking to accommodate the needs of trade. If so, then the extent to which banks borrowed to replace reserves lost through open market sales measured the true, or real bills, demand for such reserves. Open market operations themselves tested, or revealed, the extent of this demand.

Imagine that the Fed applied this test by withdrawing, via open market sales, reserves from the banking system. If banks then replenished the lost reserves through increased discount-window borrowing, this response would prove that reserves and deposits were not excessive. Reserves were not excessive because banks, in borrowing them, had to rediscount eligible paper—that is, real bills—equal to them in dollar value. That banks willingly did so was proof positive that the reserves and deposits were not excessive to the needs of trade. Only if banks failed to recoup, via rediscount of real bills, all the reserves lost through open market sales would such reserves be proved excessive. Open market operations, according to this interpretation, were hardly at odds with the Real Bills Doctrine. On the contrary, they provided a test of the doctrine's key proposition that the needs of trade constrain and determine bank credit creation.

The second interpretation, expounded by Burgess, Strong, and Riefler—which economists Karl Brunner and Allan Meltzer (1968) christened the "Riefler-Burgess Doctrine"—was the more extreme of the two. It held that open market operations could be employed to control the volume of discount-window borrowing. That is, if such borrowing varied in an inverse dollar-for-dollar ratio with open market operations as the

---

[8] On the one-for-one scissors relationship, see Yohe (1990: 483) and Meltzer (1997: 184).

scissors effect implied, then the Fed could control the former by manipulating the latter. In other words, through open market sales, the Fed could compel banks to borrow just as surely as it could, through open market purchases, spur them to pay off their indebtedness. True, the very notion of the Fed controlling discount-window activity through open market operations seemingly clashed with the passive-accommodation principle of the Real Bills Doctrine. Nevertheless, other strands of the doctrine were preserved. The Fed was still obliged to rediscount all the eligible paper offered it at any level of open market operations. Banks still eliminated their reserve deficiencies and excesses by rediscounting and repurchasing real bills at the discount window. Finally, business loan demands still drove the generation of credit and money, with the Fed supplying the necessary reserves, albeit using open market operations to nudge bank borrowing. On these grounds, at least, the doctrine was upheld.

KEY INDICATORS ESTABLISHED

The scissors effect and its interpretations helped secure the Real Bills Doctrine in the Fed Board's mindset. But they proved disastrous for the economy because they established member bank borrowing and nominal interest rates as the Fed's chief policy indicators. These misleading indicators would later flash the wrong signals at the start of the Great Depression and lead the Fed astray.

Of these indicators, high levels of member bank borrowing were taken to mean that policy was tight—tight because restrictive open market sales forced banks into the discount window in an effort to recoup the lost reserves. Conversely, low levels of member bank borrowing meant that policy was easy—easy because banks, rather than borrowing, were using abundant reserves created by expansionary open market purchases to retire discount-window indebtedness. Likewise, high nominal interest rates were taken as a sign of policy tightness as banks, reluctant to continually be in debt to the Fed, were under pressure to reduce their indebtedness.[9] To obtain funds to do so when

---

[9] Fed economists Riefler and Burgess cited a so-called tradition against borrowing or reluctance to borrow that was supposed to make banks eager to repay their indebtedness even when such borrowing was profitable. See Riefler (1930) and Burgess (1927). For a concise summary of the reluctance hypothesis, see Meltzer (1976: 464–65).

Fed contractionary policy was making reserves scarce, banks would be forced to call in outstanding loans and curtail additional lending. The resulting reduction in loan supply would raise nominal interest rates. Conversely, when borrowing was low and banks had employed plentiful reserves to repay their indebtedness, they would seek to expand their lending. The resulting expansion of loan supply relative to loan demand would put downward pressure on rates. In sum, nominal rates, varying directly with the scale of member bank borrowing, were seen as supplementing the latter as a measure of the degree of policy ease or tightness. Thus the Fed used these indicators to judge the stance of its credit and monetary policy in the late 1920s and early 1930s.

Relying on member bank borrowing and nominal rates as indicators, the Fed judged its policy to be remarkably easy in the initial phase (October 1929–December 1931) of the Great Contraction. By mid-1931, member bank borrowing and nominal rates had fallen to one-fifth and one-third, respectively, of their October 1929 levels (Wheelock 1998: 130–31, 133). By all accounts, both indicators were at extremely low levels, suggesting that the Fed already had done all it could do to arrest the contraction. Accordingly, the Fed used these indicators to justify its policy of inaction—inaction that turned what otherwise would have been a garden variety recession into the deepest depression in the nation's history. Enthralled by the Real Bills Doctrine, the Fed failed to heed alternative indicators—the money stock, the price level, *real* interest rates—all of which correctly signaled that policy was too tight. Worse, Adolph Miller and others regarded the double-digit percent contraction of the money stock, recorded in Harvard economist Lauchlin Currie's pioneering M1 series, as entirely appropriate in light of the depression's falling output and prices (Currie 1934).[10] Monetary contraction in response to cyclical declines in nominal GDP was exactly what the "needs of trade" called for. Such was the baneful legacy of the Real Bills Doctrine.

---

[10] Currie's data series were originally reported in his Harvard PhD thesis, written in 1929–1930 and submitted in January 1931. They were later confirmed by Clark Warburton in a series of journal articles published in 1945–1946, as collected in his *Depression, Inflation, and Monetary Policy, Selected Papers, 1945–1953* (Warburton 1966). See also Mints (1950: 38; 1951, 193) and Friedman and Schwartz (1963).

6

THE QUANTITY THEORY ALTERNATIVE

A singular curiosity marks the early history of the Federal Reserve. In the 1920s and early 1930s, when U.S. gold holdings were sufficiently large to relax the constraint of the international gold standard and allow domestic control of the money stock and price level, the Fed deliberately shunned the best empirical policy framework that mainstream monetary science had to offer.

Developed by Irving Fisher and other quantity theorists, this framework was the outcome of an evolution in numerical measurement that had been occurring in U.S. monetary economics since at least the early years of the 1900s. Although somewhat crude and unsophisticated by today's standards, the quantity theory framework had by the mid-1920s progressed to the point where, statistically and analytically, it was state of the art in policy analysis. Its constituent variables, all expressed in a form amenable to empirical measurement, had been fitted with relevant data series. It boasted the ability to establish empirical causality between pertinent variables, nominal and real, at cyclical and secular frequencies. It had survived rigorous testing, by the standards of the time, for accuracy and usefulness. Most of all, as the basis of a coherent and well-worked-out monetary theory of the trade cycle, it claimed to predict the effects of Fed monetary policy on output and prices in both the short run and the long. Here, ready made, seemed to be the answer to a central banker's prayers. Here was a framework the Fed could use to conduct policy to stabilize the economy.

Yet the Fed, with the exception of Benjamin Strong and a few others, refused to have anything to do with this framework and its components. Instead of concentrating on the money stock, the price level, the real rate of interest, and other variables spotlighted by the quantity theory, the Fed focused on such measures as the level of nominal market interest rates, the volume of member bank borrowing, the kinds of loans in bank loan portfolios, and the types and amounts of commercial paper eligible for rediscount at the central bank.

Why would the Fed (especially the Fed Board in Washington), seemingly in need of reliable and accurate gauges of the quantity and value of money, eschew them and the framework featuring them? Why would it deny itself the opportunity to take advantage of the improved empirical knowledge—and potential policy advances stemming therefrom—embodied in the quantity theory and its associated monetary approach to the trade cycle?

The answer, of course, was that the quantity theory framework was incompatible with the real bills–based institution created by the Federal Reserve Act of 1913. Far from the activist, price level stabilizing central bank envisioned by quantity theorists, the Fed instead was created as a passive, decentralized, noninterventionist system of 12 semiautonomous but cooperating regional reserve banks designed to accommodate productive—that is, nonspeculative—business demands for credit and money over the business cycle. The 1913 act expressly stated as much. Reserve banks, it declared, exist for the purpose of "accommodating commerce and business," a purpose they fulfill by "furnishing an elastic currency" and "affording a means of rediscounting commercial paper." Accommodation and regional autonomy were the watchwords. The act said nothing about stabilization as a policy goal or about a single monolithic agency charged with achieving that goal.

Nevertheless, by the mid-1920s more voices—some, like Benjamin Strong and Carl Snyder, from inside the Federal Reserve System, but most, like Irving Fisher and J. R. Commons, from the outside—were claiming that the Fed should have learned that active stabilization rather than passive accommodation was its overriding task and that certain statistical measures and indicators were available to help it accomplish that task. Accordingly, some of these same voices advocated amending the original Federal Reserve Act to make price stability the Fed's chief responsibility and to give power to a single central authority to unify, coordinate, and synchronize the policy actions of the individual regional reserve banks.

But the Fed—again, with the exception of Benjamin Strong at the New York regional reserve bank—rejected these suggestions and clung to the notions that accommodation was its duty and that the proffered quantity theoretic measures were both erroneous and irrelevant to discharging that duty. As a result, the Fed—particularly the Board in Washington—spurned the quantity theory or *monetary* approach in favor of an entirely different framework. Under that framework (which was based on the Real Bills Doctrine), nonmonetary forces drove the price level, while production (real output) and the associated needs of commerce determined the money stock. Based on the Real Bills Doctrine, that framework had nonmonetary forces driving the price level just as it had production (real output) and the associated needs of commerce determining the money stock.

The Fed's choice among competing policy frameworks proved momentous to its treatment of both price level and money stock changes. While the quantity theory and the Real Bills Doctrine alike saw money growth overruns or shortfalls relative to output growth as inflationary or deflationary, the Real Bills Doctrine attributed price level changes not (as in the quantity theory) to excessive or deficient aggregate spending, but rather to the *wrong kind of spending*—namely, spending for speculative as opposed to productive purposes. That is why the Fed Board hardly worried about deflation in the 1930s. To Fed real bills advocates, deflation signaled the long-awaited bursting of the speculative stock market bubble of the late 1920s. Deflation was exactly what was needed to purge the economy of the inflationary speculative excesses of that decade.

Likewise, the two frameworks yielded opposite conclusions regarding the optimum cyclical behavior of the money supply. The Real Bills Doctrine, stressing as it did that output generates the very money necessary to purchase it from the market, implies that money should vary pro-cyclically, rising with production in booms and falling with it in slumps. That is why Fed proponents of the Real Bills Doctrine could acquiesce to monetary contraction in the 1930s. To them, such contraction was entirely appropriate given the falls in output and prices that signaled the shrinking needs of trade. By contrast, the quantity theory, holding as it did that output is independent of money in long-run equilibrium but influenced strongly by it at cyclical frequencies, implied that money should vary countercyclically (or at the very least grow continually at the economy's trend rate of output growth) in the interest of economic stabilization. To quantity theorists, monetary contraction was the worst possible treatment for a slump. Had the Fed adhered to this view rather than to the real bills framework, the Great Depression arguably would have been avoided.

KEY ELEMENTS OF THE QUANTITY THEORY OF MONEY

The distinguishing characteristic of the quantity theory framework that vied unsuccessfully for the Fed Board's acceptance in the first 25 years of the system's existence is easily described. It consisted of a causal chain running from Fed policy to bank reserves to the broad money stock and thence to general prices and real output. It implied that the Fed could control the money stock and thereby stabilize prices and smooth the business cycle. By the mid-1920s a vigorous empirical tradition had developed in the United States around the quantity theory framework. Indeed, this strong empirical orientation was the hallmark of American quantity theorists, whose use of statistical data to test and illustrate the theory went far beyond the efforts of their University of Cambridge and continental European counterparts. Key figures in this tradition included Simon Newcomb, John Pease Norton, Edwin W. Kemmerer, Irving Fisher, Warren M. Persons, Carl Snyder, and Holbrook Working.

It was Newcomb, a renowned astronomer and part-time economist who, in his 1885 *Principles of Political Economy*, suggested that David Ricardo's $P = MV/T$ equation of exchange—which expressed the price level P as the product of the stock of money M and its circulation velocity V per unit of real transactions T—might serve as an empirical framework to examine money's effects on the economy.[1] Newcomb also suggested that the total stock of circulating media could be divided into its separate coin, paper currency, and demand deposit components, each with its own velocity coefficient, an idea that Norton, in his 1902 *Statistical Studies in the New York Money Market*, developed into the most comprehensive, disaggregated version of the equation of exchange ever published.[2] Inspired by Newcomb, Kemmerer, in his 1907 *Money and Credit Instruments in Their Relation to General Prices*, and Fisher, in his 1911 *The Purchasing Power of Money*, elaborated on Newcomb's suggestions in several ways.

Kemmerer and Fisher incorporated variables representing checking deposits M' and their velocity V' into the equation to obtain $P = (MV + M'V')/T$ where M denotes coin and currency and V its turnover velocity. Then, after constructing independent data series of index numbers for each of the equation's elements, they consolidated these separate series into a single series for the entire right-hand side of the equation. The resulting magnitude, $(MV + M'V')/T$, gave them an estimated or predicted value of the price level P, which they then compared with an independent price index series representing the actual observed price level.[3] Here was their statistical test of the quantity theory proposition that velocity times money (cash plus checking deposits) per unit of trade determines the price level.

Visually comparing graphed curves of the two price series over the period 1878–1901, Kemmerer concluded that the fit, or degree of correspondence, between the curves, passed the ocular test closely enough to verify the quantity theory. Persons (1908: 289) challenged this conclusion by calculating the correlation coefficient for the two curves as a meager 0.23 with a probable error of 0.13. Fisher (1913: 294) countered by computing the correlation coefficient for the updated period

---

[1] Ricardo stated the $P = MV/T$ equation as follows: "Put the mass of commodities of all sorts [T] on one side of the line—and the amount of money [M] multiplied by the rapidity of its circulation [V] on the other. Is not this in all cases the regulator of prices [P]?" See Ricardo ([1810–1811] 1951: 311).

[2] Besides containing separate terms for each type of coin and currency in circulation and their respective velocities, Norton's equation included notation representing bank reserves, the deposit expansion multiplier, the proportion of maximum allowable deposits actually created, and the discounted and full maturity values of bank loans—all for the four classes of banks existing in the United States in 1902.

[3] Fisher's observed price level series was a weighted average of the prices of 258 commodities, labor hourly wage rates, and prices of 40 stocks.

1896–1909. The coefficient registered a high 0.97 value, indicating a very close fit.

Further support for Fisher came when he and Persons applied advanced techniques of trend removal to Fisher's original series (Fisher 1913: 295; Persons 1911: 827–28). Doing so, they found that the correlation remained respectably high even after the series were cleansed of serial correlation. Fisher also found that discrepancies between the actual and predicted price series forecast the direction of movement of the former as it gravitated to the latter. Fisher argued that, together, these findings verified the quantity theory.

Nevertheless, critics such as Benjamin Anderson (1917) contended that Fisher's work (and Kemmerer's too) consisted merely of attempts to confirm the equation of exchange rather than the quantity theory. Critics further maintained that because the equation is a mere accounting identity—and with its velocity term defined as $V = PT/M$ a tautologically truistic one at that—accurate measurement of its constituent variables could result in no disparity between the predicted and actual price levels that constituted the opposite sides of the equation. If so, then high correlation between the two price series indicates merely the absence of measurement error rather than the validity of the quantity theory.

Countering this criticism, Fisher argued that the equation, far from being an identity, is an equilibrium condition expressed as a functional relationship $P = f(M, V, T) = MV/T$ in which the independent variables M, V, and T "tend to *bring about* a determined value of P, but do not simply *spell* a certain P," in the words of Joseph Schumpeter (1954: 1096). This independence-of-variables equilibrium interpretation of the equation allowed Fisher to contend, contrary to critics like Anderson, that the price level indeed is determined by velocity times money per unit of real output just as the quantity theory held. That is, he claimed that with velocity defined independently of the other variables so that the equation becomes nontautological, the price level adjusts to equate the real or price-deflated money stock M/P to the real demand for it, this real demand being the fraction $1/V$ of real transactions T the public wishes to hold in the form of real cash balances.

With the empirical quantity equation in place, New York Fed statistician Carl Snyder—that rarest of birds, a Fed quantity theorist—and University of Minnesota economist Holbrook Working applied it in an effort to establish the direction of causation between money (defined by them as demand deposits) and prices at secular and cyclical frequencies.[4] Secularly, they found the long-run path of prices to be determined jointly by the trend rates of growth of money, velocity, and trade. Of those trend growth rates, they found velocity's to be approximately 0 percent per annum whereas trade's was approximately 4 percent. They concluded that the money stock must expand secularly at the 4 percent trend growth rate to stabilize the price level.

In short, Snyder and Working had established that with velocity trendless, the price level evolves secularly at the differential growth rates of money and trade. But when Snyder examined the cyclical or deviation-from-trend behavior of the quantity-theory variables, he claimed to have found that fluctuations in velocity entirely accommodated fluctuations in trade such that the ratio of those variables remained a fixed constant over the cycle. With V/T fixed in the short run at its long-run trend value, he concluded that money causes prices contemporaneously at every point of the cycle.

Working, however, realized that things could not possibly be that simple. His data series told him that while money did indeed determine prices over the cycle, it did so with a lag rather than contemporaneously. In his interpretation, the resulting lagged adjustment of prices to money necessitated compensating cyclical changes in the velocity-to-trade ratio to keep the exchange equation in balance. In other words, the ratio, far from adhering continuously to its trend equilibrium level, exhibits transitory deviations from trend with temporarily sticky prices accounting for the deviations. Due to temporarily inflexible prices, monetary shocks initially disturbed the ratio, driving it from equilibrium. But with inflexibility quickly vanishing,

---

[4] See Snyder (1924: 699, 710) and Working (1923: 228–56; 1926: 120–33).

corrective price level changes subsequently eliminated the deviation and restored the ratio to trend.

To estimate the lead-lag relationship between money and prices corresponding to this result, Working (1923: 1926) correlated detrended money with contemporaneous and lagged prices. He found that such correlations, though high for all lag lengths up to a year, were highest at six to eight months. This result was roughly consistent with his findings from direct comparison of cyclical turning points of money and prices. There he found that trend-adjusted money not only consistently led or preceded prices in all 19 pairs of turning points examined, but did so with an average lead time of 12 months at the lower turning points and nine months at the upper ones. Here seemed to be strong evidence of temporal money-to-price causality.

REAL EFFECTS IN IRVING FISHER'S QUANTITY THEORETIC TRADE CYCLE

To Working's analysis of money's cyclical price level effects, Fisher added his seminal and incisive account of the output and employment effects. In essence, Fisher equipped the framework with a Phillips-curve tradeoff relationship between output and surprise (i.e., unexpected) inflation. He used the relationship to argue that unanticipated price changes caused by monetary shocks were responsible for fluctuations in real interest rates and, through those real rate movements, in output and employment as well. Towering above the rest, his empirical contributions to the monetary theory of the cycle are to be found in his three remarkable journal articles of the mid-1920s (Fisher 1923: 1925, 1926). But he had already sketched out the underlying theory in his classic 1911 book *The Purchasing Power of Money*.

There he argued that although money stock changes have no permanent, enduring effects on real output and employment, they do influence those variables temporarily over periods lasting as long as 10 years. To account for these transitory real effects, Fisher appealed to two concepts first enunciated in his 1896 monograph "Appreciation and Interest"—namely, the distinction between real and nominal interest rates and the notion of asymmetrical expectations between business borrowers and bank lenders (Fisher 1896). The first concept defines the real rate of interest as the observed nominal market interest rate minus the expected rate of price inflation or deflation. The second concept says that business borrowers, by virtue of their far-seeing entrepreneurial skill, possess superior foresight and so anticipate and therefore adjust to inflation and deflation faster than do bank lenders. According to Fisher, inflation, being accurately anticipated and perceived, lowers the real rate as seen by business borrowers. Bankers, however, being slower than their customers to adjust their inflationary expectations, see a higher real rate. Deflation works analogously to raise the real rate seen by borrowers above the real rate seen by bankers.

Fisher (1913: 55–73) attributed business cycles to such real rate movements. Imagine that an increase in the money stock sets prices rising. Because nominal market interest rates (reflecting the inferior foresight of bankers) adjust more slowly to inflation than do the expectations of entrepreneurs, real rates seen by the latter group fall. (Similarly, real wage, rent, and raw material costs also fall as their nominal values fail to adjust to inflation as fast as do the expectations of entrepreneurs.) Such real rate falls, boosting as they do the expected rate of profit on bank loan-financed business projects, spur corresponding increases in investment, output, and employment. As the expansion proceeds, banks run up against their reserve constraints. Moreover, banks begin to lose reserves when depositors, who need additional coin and currency to mediate a rising volume of hand-to-hand payments, withdraw cash from their checking accounts (and so force, in a fractional reserve banking system, a multiple contraction of deposits). To protect their reserves from such cash drains, banks raise their nominal loan rate until it catches up with and then surpasses the increased rate of inflation. Real rates rise, thereby precipitating the downturn. Causation runs from money to prices to real interest rates to output and employment.

Having sketched his theory, Fisher next sought its empirical verification. Citing Working's 1923 estimate that money stock changes over the period 1890–1921 had led price level changes by about eight months, he took this finding as constituting strong evidence of money-to-price causality (Fisher 1925: 199). To establish corresponding price-to-output causality, he correlated distributed lags in the rates of price change with an index of the physical volume of trade. Likewise, to establish price-to-employment causality, he correlated distributed lags in the rates of price change and employment. Finding a high correlation of 0.941 for the first set of series and 0.90 for the second, he concluded that "the ups and downs of [output and] employment are the effects . . . of the rises and falls of prices, due in turn to the inflation and deflation of money and credit" (Fisher 1926: 792).[5]

Here was his statistical confirmation of the trade cycle as a monetary phenomenon receptive to a monetary cure. Cycles, in other words, stem from price level movements caused by misbehavior of the money stock. It follows that monetary policy, properly conducted, could stabilize the price level and in so doing eliminate the business cycle as well. Policymakers simply had to observe and react to the price level. Its deviations from target would trigger corrective monetary responses that would restore it to target. The price level itself formed the main gauge of monetary policy. If policymakers desired supplementary indicators of monetary tightness or ease, they could observe the money stock and real interest rates—the remaining chief variables of Fisher's version of the quantity theoretic framework.

FISHER'S PROPOSED IMPROVEMENT TO THE GOLD STANDARD

Having shown how price level changes provoke cyclical swings in real activity, Fisher sought a remedy for those swings. He found it in his famous "compensated dollar" proposal for stabilizing domestic prices under the gold standard. His plan called for a monetary authority to adjust the dollar price of gold opposite to movements in the world gold price of goods, as approximated empirically by changes in the

---

[5] Fisher employed at least three weighting schemes to distribute the lag. The first used linearly declining monthly weights for eight-month intervals. The second used a unimodal sequence of lag coefficients to weight past rates of price change. The third and most ambitious scheme distributed the lag according to the density function of a lognormal distribution (see Chipman 1999: 192–94). All schemes yielded high correlation coefficients.

preceding month's general price index, so as to keep domestic prices constant.[6]

Fisher thought his plan was consistent with both the quantity theory and the gold standard. He was wrong on the latter score.[7] The traditional gold standard cannot tolerate any management by authorities. It takes care of itself automatically through market adjustments. Especially, it bars manipulation of the dollar price of gold, which is a constitutionally fixed constant. Fisher's plan was incompatible with a true gold standard.

CLOSING OBSERVATIONS

Fisher's quantity theoretic cycle model spotlighted the money stock, price level, and real interest rate as policy indicators. It linked these indicators through a causal chain running from the Fed to real activity, with the Fed initiating the causal sequence. The Fed determined the money stock. The money stock determined the price level. The rate of change of the price level temporarily moved the real rate of interest. Movements of the real rate influenced output and employment. The cycle admitted to both a monetary cause and a monetary cure. The Fed, by stabilizing the price level, could also smooth the cycle.

However, economists and officials at the Federal Reserve Board in the 1920s and 1930s rejected this model. Instead, they adhered to the Real Bills Doctrine, in which causation runs in the opposite direction from prices and real activity to money, with the Fed occupying a passive, accommodative role (Laidler 1999: 18; Yohe 1990: 486). In the Fed Board's real bills framework, seasonal and cyclical movements in real activity drive business demands for bank loans. Because banks supply such loans in the form of newly created check-deposit money subject to

[6] In symbols $P = GW$, where P is the dollar price of goods (the domestic U.S. price level), G the official dollar price of gold, and W the world gold price of goods. Changes in G offset changes in W to keep P stable.

[7] His plan was consistent with the quantity theory, as changes in the dollar price of gold moved the monetary gold base as well as the stock of broad money and the price level it supported in the desired direction. For example, a lowering, or cheapening, of gold's price would shunt the metal from monetary into nonmonetary, industrial uses. At the same time, it would shrink the dollar value of monetary gold reserves and so the volume of broad money erected thereupon. Through physical reduction and nominal devaluation, the monetary gold base would shrink and so too the stock of broad money and the price level.

a fixed fractional reserve requirement, these same movements lead to corresponding changes in bank demands for reserves—reserves borrowed from the Fed. The Fed passively accommodates these demands by discounting bank paper of acceptable quality (i.e., real bills). In so doing, it contributes seasonal and cyclical elasticity to the money stock.

As the following chapters will show, however, the flawed real bills framework proved disastrous in the 1930s Great Depression. At that time the doctrine's prescribed monetary contraction was the exact opposite of what was required. By contrast, the rejected quantity theoretic framework would have prescribed the right medicine to prevent the depression.

7

THE NEW YORK FED'S STABLE PRICE LEVEL POLICY, 1922–1929

Under the operating world gold standard between 1898 and 1914, and even earlier, prices were very stable, as were most other financial conditions. One of the characteristics of such a period is the absence of any serious or pervasive speculation. However, wartime fiscal policies of the nations embroiled in World War I interrupted this happy time. All the warring countries went off the gold standard, substituting national legal tender paper moneys for gold, much like the United States had done in 1862–1863 during the Civil War. The inevitable result was inflation of various magnitudes throughout Europe and, to a lesser degree, in the United States. Prices in all countries rose by varying percentages. After the 1918 armistice, peaceful conditions returned, and national governments tried to dis-inflate their currencies and return to the gold standard.

But none was able to achieve the real value its money had had in 1914. The trading world was not accustomed to the kind of volatility that appeared in the postwar monetary systems—first, inflations of significant magnitudes, then similar deflations. Such nominal price changes had not occurred since the Napoleonic era a hundred years earlier.

Beginning in 1918 and continuing into the 1920s, as markets reacted to varying demands and supplies, price speculation in many goods and services burgeoned. Real prices, adjusted for changes in the value of the moneys current, went up and down as usual, but money prices (which included changes in real prices plus the nominal price effects from variable wartime monetary excesses) fluctuated much more. This volatile price environment encouraged speculation in many markets.

While speculation is a necessary and almost ubiquitous practice in the formation of virtually all market prices, at that time it also had an aura of immorality. It became an object of opprobrium in virtually all discussions of monetary policy. No one had a good word for speculation. It reflected overindulgence, such as alcoholism, overeating, or some other dissipation.[1]

Speculation also fostered an anti-speculation mentality, especially in the minds of real bills advocates of the time. Real bills were not speculative. They reflected the real values of the real goods that gave rise to the real bills. Furthermore, if banks dealt only in real bills, speculation and its accompanying uncertainty would be minimized. It was a short step for proponents of the Real Bills Doctrine to apply this principle to the monetary policy of the Federal Reserve System.

A monetary policy that ignored the quality of loans while focusing on their quantity was unacceptable to the proponents of the Real Bills Doctrine. Such an approach could only apply to a system in which the quantity of money was determined by central banking policies. It therefore violated the key element in the Real Bills Doctrine, in which productive initiatives (in the form of real bills) generated "credit" and money. It also was inapplicable under a gold standard. A gold standard, while it could tolerate a Real Bills Doctrine, determined the economy's quantity of money through the entire system of markets. No institution or persons could deliberately design a monetary "policy" under a gold standard (see Girton and Roper 1978). The gold standard, however, even after the Recession of 1920–1922, was inoperative. That is, it was still on the books but not viable—on hold until the rest of the trading world's chaotic monetary affairs, left over from World War I, could be undone or made operational again.

---

[1] From an account of a 1920 discussion among Federal Reserve bank governors and members of the Federal Reserve Board:

"Most of the Reserve Banks, through circular letters and other methods, urged member banks not to make loans for speculative activities, such as in securities or to enable borrowers to hold commodities for higher prices. The Governor of one of the Reserve Banks stated that borrowing to buy automobiles was one of the most extravagant things they had to cope with and that people were buying cars who could not afford them. One Reserve Bank refused to discount paper arising from the sale of pleasure automobiles, on the basis that the industry was overextended. The policy was soon abandoned, however."

This quotation is from a paper by Clay Anderson at the Federal Reserve Bank of Philadelphia: C. J. Anderson, "Evolution of the Role and the Functioning of the Discount Mechanism," in *Reappraisal of the Federal Reserve Discount Mechanism*, vol. 1 (Washington: Board of Governors of the Federal Reserve System, 1971), 133–63.

Up to 1922, the Federal Reserve banks had not undertaken many initiatives. All of their activities between 1914 and 1920 had been to expedite and support the Treasury's wartime fiscal policies. Consequently, most officers in Fed banks wondered just what they ought to be doing as the touted lenders of last resort when there were no money market problems. Unlike the clearinghouse associations, they could not pack up their loan certificates and simply be commercial banks again once a monetary panic had passed. They were an *institution* and had to figure out something to *do*.

It was under these conditions that Benjamin Strong, who had been appointed governor of the Federal Reserve Bank of New York in 1914, became the leading spokesman for a particular Fed policy. Before joining the Fed, Strong had been secretary of the Bankers Trust Company, one of the most prestigious banks in New York City. During the 1907 crisis, he also had been chairman of one of the clearinghouse committees that was supposed to "determine which institutions could be saved and to appraise the collateral they offered as loans" (Chandler 1958: 460). This experience served him well in the system that had taken over both the clearing and countercyclical policies of the clearinghouses. Strong had the counsel of Irving Fisher, probably the most learned and professionally accomplished economist of the day, who was practically an evangelist in support of a policy of price level stabilization. Strong also had the leading price index economist of the time, Carl Snyder, on his staff, which suggests that constancy of prices was reasonably well understood if not wholeheartedly endorsed.[2]

Strong expressed his views on price stabilization in an article he wrote but did not publish in 1923.[3] In the article Strong showed a professional understanding of prices, the price level, and the two items—hand-to-hand currency and banks' demand deposit balance—that made up the quantity of money.

[2] Snyder was important for three monetary and price discoveries or innovations. First was his finding that with velocity trendless, money must grow at trade's 4 percent trend growth rate to preserve secular price stability. Second was his empirical finding that the trend-adjusted ratio V/T of velocity-to-trade was a fixed constant over the cycle. To Snyder this finding meant that money determined prices at every point in the cycle. Third was his inclusive general price index number constructed from the prices of commodities, labor, real estate, bonds, and stocks. Strong was somewhat less enthusiastic about Snyder's second finding.

[3] The article, "Prices and Price Controls," appears in Burgess ([1930] 1983: 224–34).

"There are," he wrote, "two distinct points of outstanding importance to keep in mind in considering prices: one is the general price level and its changes; the other is the variation in the relative prices of different things . . . [all of] which may take place at the same time, including wages and commodities." What we want, Strong wrote, ". . . is a reasonably stable general price level." He then noted that prices "are influenced to advance or decline by increases or decreases in the total of 'money' in circulation." He included in "money" hand-to-hand currency and bank deposits. The Federal Reserve's significant control over the quantity of money, he stated, gave it the power to determine the price level. While he denied that monetary policy should fix prices, he nevertheless argued that "the writer . . . maintains that the task of the System is to maintain a reasonably stable volume of money and credit, with due allowances for seasonal fluctuations in demand, [and] for normal annual growth in the country's development, business and population" (Burgess [1930] 1983: 227–30).

From this 1923 article, it is abundantly clear that Strong was at least a 95 percent quantity theorist and that he would use the Fed's powers over the money stock to maintain something close to 95 percent price stability.

Throughout the 1920s, Strong's position as governor of the New York Fed made him virtual chancellor of Federal Reserve policy. In that capacity he wrote several papers on policy, met with the heads of European central banks, gave advice to congressional committees, and made many appearances before other audiences who were interested in the role of the newly created Federal Reserve System.[4]

By virtue of his personality and the natural dominance of the New York Fed in the financial system, Strong was able to initiate a stable price level policy beginning in 1922, after the economy had recovered from the sharp recession of 1919–1921. His principal means of monetary control was open market operations in government securities. Several Fed banks accepted this method for Fed policy and formed a

[4] Strong's salary was about $50,000 a year—the kind of money a corporate executive could command. By way of contrast, the secretary of the Treasury made $12,000 a year, and Fed Board members made around $8,000.

more formal Open Market Investment Committee, with Strong as its permanent chairman, to provide this policy for the Federal Reserve System as a whole. Of course, the New York bank as well as the other Fed banks continued their other financial activities.

The New York Fed maintained the stable price level policy from 1922 until some months after Strong's death in late 1928 (Chandler 1958: 194–206).[5] During that seven-year period, 1922 to mid-1929 and most of 1930, the average of money prices, as measured by any price index, was as stable as at any time in U.S. history.[6] At the same time, business and the economy prospered—so much so that some contemporary observers referred to the good times as a "stable price level boom." Indeed, the stock market did register a "boom," but the average of money prices of all goods and services in all markets was remarkably steady. The Consumer Price Index (CPI) value was 71.6 in June 1922 and 71.4 in June 1930, eight years later—as shown in Table 1. The Fed under Strong became, for the time being, a quantity theory of money Federal Reserve System.[7]

Despite the success of Strong's policies during the 1920s, speculation, especially in the New York stock market, became more and more a moralistic no-no. Real bills advocates regarded speculation as the most important problem facing monetary policy. But Strong, whether or not he thought speculation evil, argued that Federal Reserve policy could do nothing about it. In a paper presented to students of the Harvard Business School in November 1922, he noted:

> When a member bank's reserve balance is impaired, it borrows [from a Fed bank] to make it good, and it is quite impossible to determine to what particular purpose the money so borrowed [will] be applied. . . . [It] makes little difference to the borrowing bank what transactions may have caused the impairment of its reserve, because the paper which it discounts at the Reserve Bank may have no relation whatever to the impairment that has

---

[5] See also Friedman and Schwartz (1963: 411) and Hetzel (2008).

[6] Sometimes economists used other indexes to measure general prices (Burgess 1927: 281).

[7] For an account of Strong's policies in the 1920s, see Burgess [1930] (1983).

TABLE 1

Behavior of Money and Prices, 1921–1934

YEAR	MONETARY BASE MB (1)	MONEY STOCK M1 (2)	FED RESERVE MONETARY LIABILITIES FRL (3)	FED RESERVE GOLD AND OTHER ASSETS RG (4)	FED RESERVE NET LIABILITIES MNL (3) − (4)	YEAR-TO-YEAR CHANGE IN NET LIABILITIES ΔMNL	REAL BILLS BOUGHT AND DISCOUNTED B	PRICES (CPI=100, 1947–1949)
1921	6.55	21.0	4.79	2.63	2.16	.....	1.09	76.4
1922	6.32	21.6	4.29	3.09	1.20	−0.96	0.98	71.6
1923	6.68	22.7	4.24	3.17	1.07	−0.13	0.89	72.9
1924	6.85	23.2	4.12	3.11	1.01	−0.06	0.86	73.1
1925	6.95	25.4	4.07	2.94	1.13	0.12	1.02	75.0
1926	7.13	26.1	4.05	2.89	1.16	0.03	1.00	75.6
1927	7.24	25.8	4.16	2.91	1.25	0.09	1.26	74.2
1928	7.15	25.8	4.26	2.79	1.47	0.22	1.29	73.3
1929	7.10	26.2	4.25	2.86	1.39	−0.08	0.82	73.3
1930	6.91	25.3	4.21	3.05	1.16	−0.23	0.80	71.4
1931	7.30	23.9	4.36	3.12	1.24	0.08	0.62	65.0
1932	7.79	20.5	4.92	3.24	1.68	0.44	0.25	58.4
1933	7.94	19.2	5.63	3.56	2.07	0.39	0.12	55.3
1934	9.26	21.1	6.68	4.60	2.08	0.01	0.01	57.2
Change 1921–1930	0.36	4.30	−0.58	0.42	−1.00	---	−0.29	−5.00%
Change 1928–1934	0.79	−6.60	1.37	0.77	0.60	---	−1.17	−32%

Sources: Monetary Base and M1 are from Friedman and Schwartz (1963: 801–4, 709–14; Tables B-3 and A-1). Fed banks' balance-sheet data are from Board of Governors (1943: 330–32). Price index values are from U.S. Census Bureau (1960: 125, Series E-113).

arisen. . . . Suppose a member bank's reserve became impaired solely because . . . it had made a number of loans on the stock exchange; it might then come to us with commercial paper, . . . which had no relation whatever to the transactions of the day; and with the proceeds of the discount make good the impairment. . . . And surely it cannot be claimed that the provisions of the [Federal Reserve] Act, which specify so exactly what paper is eligible, can possibly have exercised any influence upon the application of the proceeds of these loans by member banks. . . . The eligible paper we discount is simply the vehicle through which the credit of the Reserve System is conveyed to the members. . . . The definition of eligibility does not effect the slightest control over the use to which the proceeds are applied. . . . [The] eligible paper may have had its origin in any sort of expansive development, stock speculation, real estate speculation, crop moving, foreign bond issues, or anything else. (Burgess [1930] 1983: 182–84)

In spite of his understanding of the relation of the economy's stock of money to the general price level, and *the* monetary policy he promoted for most of the 1920s, Strong's first priority was to get the United States, and the rest of the trading world, back on the gold standard. He recognized that in such a system, no policy of price stabilization would be appropriate or possible. Prices might well stay reasonably stable under a gold standard. But since the gold standard was the monetary policy, no institution, such as a central bank, could tamper with it. Any central bank in the presence of a formal, operational gold standard can be nothing more than a lender of last resort.

When Rep. James Strong of Kansas introduced a bill in 1926 to direct the Fed to use its powers toward price level stabilization, Fed Governor Strong opposed it. Representative Strong then revised the bill and brought it up again in 1928. During the hearing on the revised bill (March 19, 1928), Governor Strong—while expressing his approval of the ideal of price level stability—opposed the revised bill as well. First, he believed that other factors—besides the volume of money and credit—control prices. Second, he feared that a stable price level policy might lead the public to believe the bill was meant to fix individual commodity prices, rather than to maintain a statistical average of prices. He recognized the inherent discordance between a monetary policy aimed at maintaining price stability and the spontaneous operations of the international gold standard. He also thought that a restored gold standard would accomplish everything anticipated by the stable price level bill (Burgess [1930] 1983: 326).

Representative Strong wanted language written into the law "to direct that the powers placed in [Fed managers'] hands shall continue to be used toward promoting the stability of the purchasing power of the dollar" (Burgess [1930] 1983: 327). Governor Strong replied that the main problem probably would be inflation, and that the primary hedge against either inflation or deflation would be the traditional gold standard (Burgess [1930] 1983: 328–29).

The representative in charge of the hearing, Otis Wingo, then asked rhetorically, "What is there in our experience as a people to say that a political [Federal Reserve] board sitting at Washington can tell anyone in this country how more efficiently to conduct his business?" Governor Strong replied:

> That question is really applicable to the last few questions in this questionnaire. Again getting back to the gold standard, the gold standard is a much more automatic check upon excesses in credit and currency than is a system where gold payment . . . is suspended and it is left to the human judgment of men to determine how much currency shall be issued which they do not have to redeem in gold. . . . And when you speak of a gold standard you are speaking of something where the limitation upon judgment is exact and precise and the penalty for bad judgment is immediate. (Burgess [1930] 1983: 331)

This testimony in support of a true gold standard was the last such activity Strong would make. He died some months later in October 1928.

Meanwhile, without regard to Strong's stable price level policy, security prices, particularly those of common stocks, were rising rapidly, reflecting the promising course of postwar business enterprise. Along with the results of productive enterprise, as would be expected, came a moralistic movement in real bills circles against "speculation." In fact, speculation in security purchases is simply a part of routine anticipation of uncertain future incomes. Speculation can never be absent from such dealings: Anticipation of uncertain future income is necessarily speculative in varying degrees. Investment without any speculation is both undesirable and impossible.

The anti-speculative movement in the 1920s, however, became pervasive. It had many influential members, some of the most important of whom were the real bills advocates in the Federal Reserve System, and particularly some members of the Federal Reserve Board. After Strong's death, the New York bank lost its systemwide leadership to the Board in Washington.[8]

Some Fed officials, guided by their real bills heritage, were much opposed to Strong's stable price level policies. They neither wanted the Fed to do such things, nor thought that it should or even could. Their concern was to counter speculation, especially in financial markets, so that Fed policy could accommodate real bills principles and in so doing reject any efforts to stabilize price levels.

One of those who openly objected to Strong's stable price level policy was Adolph C. Miller, a longtime member of the Federal Reserve Board. Woodrow Wilson had appointed Miller to the original Board of Governors in 1914, and Calvin Coolidge reappointed him in 1924. Miller and the other members of the Fed Board were outspoken critics both of the policymaking powers of the New York Fed and, especially, Strong's price stabilizing open market operations. Miller was the quintessential "real billser." He was a student, friend, and colleague of J. Laurence Laughlin, the intellectual leader of the Real Bills

---

[8] For a complete discussion of this shift in emphasis, see Friedman and Schwartz (1963: 290–98, 362–74, and passim).

Doctrine in the United States (Bornemann 1940: 26).[9] Also in the Laughlin circle was H. Parker Willis, who studied under Laughlin at the University of Chicago. Laughlin was a longtime opponent of the quantity theory of money, and Willis and Miller actively supported his views.[10] Miller received a master's degree in economics under Laughlin's direction, and Willis earned a PhD.

A fourth member of this group, who became the political spokesman for the Real Bills Doctrine in Congress, was Carter Glass, first a representative and then a senator from Virginia. Glass was chairman of the House Committee on Banking and Currency that drafted the Federal Reserve Act in 1912–1913 and, after he became a senator, chairman of the Senate Finance Committee until 1936. Willis taught economics to Glass's children at Washington and Lee University around 1905 and became Glass's principal adviser in the writing of the Federal Reserve Act. During 1918–1920, Miller was a prominent member of the Fed Board; Glass was secretary of the Treasury and, therefore, chairman of the Fed Board, and Willis was secretary of the Board (Bornemann 1940: 27–31, 51–59). This group of real bills proponents complained often but unsuccessfully about Strong's price level stabilization policy. But after Strong's death in 1928, proponents of the Real Bills Doctrine at the Fed's Board of Governors in Washington managed to get control of both the Board and monetary policy.

[9] Laughlin was the first head of the economics department at the University Chicago. Friedman and Schwartz (1963: 417n178) cite another member of the Board, Charles Hamlin, who authored a diary in which he wrote that Miller "was a self-centered person, with little hesitation in using his public position for personal advantage, and capable of shifting his position on important issues for trivial reasons."

[10] Laughlin earned a PhD in history from Harvard. While he had no formal economics training at Harvard, he learned some principles of economics when he studied under Charles Dunbar, one of the profession's first economists.

8

THE REAL BILLS DOCTRINE IN THE
GREAT CONTRACTION, 1929–1933

In February 1929, just a few months after Benjamin Strong's death in October 1928, Adolph C. Miller became the driving intellectual force behind Fed policy. He had publicly criticized Strong and the New York Fed on a number of occasions, although Strong had successfully countered Miller's sniping. Miller was never chairman of the Fed Board, but through his dogmatic persistence in promoting the Real Bills Doctrine over his many years there, he came to intellectually dominate the other Board members and its policies. Fortunately for the record, Miller wrote a detailed journal article on the entire episode of the Fed's monetary contraction from 1929 to 1933. His article was published in the *American Economic Review* in 1935. In it Miller explained in detail the Fed's anti-speculation policy for the years 1929–1933 and his role in promoting it (Miller 1935a).[1]

Besides loathing the quantity theory of money, Miller's particular aversion as a policymaker was to speculation—principally speculation in the stock market, which was a real bills no-no. He was able to convince a majority of the other eight members of the Board in early 1929 that something had to be done to restrain this sinful practice—not only because everybody and his grandmother were engaged in it, but also because speculation was not "productive." Accordingly, in February 1929, under Miller's guidance, the Board unleashed an evangelical crusade against speculation—particularly against commercial banks that were accommodating the lending frenzy in the stock market.

In his article reviewing the contraction period (1929–1933), Miller charged that Strong's policies in the presence of stock market speculation "proved to be unequal to the situation . . . in this period of optimism gone

---

[1] This article is a shorter version of extended testimony Miller (1935b) gave to the House Banking and Currency Committee on June 24, 1935.

wild and cupidity gone drunk" (Miller 1935a: 453). The Fed Board's "anxiety," he continued, "reached a point where [the Board] felt that it must assume the responsibility for intervening . . . in the speculative situation menacing the welfare of the country." Consequently, on February 2, 1929, the Board sent a policy letter, crafted mostly by Miller, to all the Fed banks stating that the Board had the "duty . . . to restrain the use of Federal Reserve credit facilities in aid of the growth of speculative credit." To accomplish that end, the letter continued, the Board was initiating a policy of "direct pressure" that restricted borrowings from the Federal Reserve banks "by those member banks which were increasingly disposed to lend funds for speculative purposes" (Miller 1935a: 454).[2]

Direct pressure added a major obstacle to member banks' borrowing over and above the cost to them of a discount rate. "It put the member bank," Miller noted approvingly, ". . . under pressure by obliging it to show that it was entitled to accommodation. . . . It was a method of exercising discriminating control over the extension of Federal Reserve credit such as the purely technical and impartial method of [Fed] bank [discount] rate could not do" (Miller 1935a: 455–56).

Monetary historian Clark Warburton, writing some 15 years later, recounted the viciousness of direct pressure:

> In the early 1930s [Fed banks] virtually stopped rediscounting or otherwise acquiring "eligible" paper. This [cessation] was not due to any lack of eligible paper. . . . Throughout 1930, 1931, and 1932 . . . the amount of member bank borrowings was [only] about [25 to 40 percent] the magnitude of 1928 and 1929 and remained at about [5 to 10 percent] of the eligible paper held by member banks. . . . [It] was due to strenuous discouragement of continuous discounting by any member bank, "direct pressure" so strong as to amount to a virtual prohibition of rediscounting for banks which were making loans for security speculation, and a "hard-boiled" attitude toward banks in special need of rediscounts because of deposit withdrawals. (Warburton 1966: 339–40)

[2] The letter was made public on February 7, 1929. In subsequent reference to this policy, many observers used the term "direct action."

Direct pressure subjected the borrowing bank to an inquisition on its lending policies, meant to discourage the applicant. It made the formal discount rate almost meaningless. A bank not able to pass the direct pressure test could not borrow from a Fed bank at any rate, no matter how much good paper it had, or how badly it needed credit to meet deposit withdrawals. The unofficial discount rate for a "guilty" bank effectively became infinite. In Miller's words, "'Direct pressure' works as the name indicates, by direct control of *member banks* instead of indirectly through money rates" (Miller 1935b: 27). The phrase "control of member banks" is by itself an indictment of the direct pressure policy. It overtly implies that the Board could destroy the "speculative" *member banks*. And, indeed, that is precisely what it did.

To a client bank, discretion by authority now substituted for the objective Fed discount rate as a means to ration Federal Reserve credit. Direct pressure also contradicted the positive prescriptions for Fed bank discounting set forth in the Federal Reserve Act and thereby violated the very Real Bills Doctrine that had played such an important role in the construction of the act. Even if a needy bank had real bills to discount, its sin of lending in some capacity for stock market activity would, under the direct pressure constraint, subvert its legitimate needs.

Miller had little modesty about who was responsible for the new restrictive policy:

> It is not without significance that the five members [out of nine] of the board [including himself] who took the responsibility of formulating the policy and attitude of the federal reserve system were opposed by a minority [four] of their own membership, including the Secretary of the Treasury, the governor and vice-governor of the Board, by the [presidents of] the twelve federal reserve banks, the Federal Advisory Council, and by many of the largest member banks. . . . Nonetheless, the Board adhered to its position. (Miller 1935b: 456)[3]

---

[3] If any event emphasized the possibility of unconstitutional imbalance of majoritarian policy, it was this one. Virtually every Federal Reserve official disagreed with the "direct pressure" policy. The five-man majority on the Fed Board, however, was a "majority" and could not be dissuaded.

Several aspects of Miller and the Board's action during the Great Contraction of 1929–1933 are notable for historical accuracy and have implications for subsequent policies.

First, nowhere in Miller's *American Economic Review* article is there any serious, or even casual, mention of the gold standard—whether it was working, how it should work, how it could be restored to its proper role, or anything else. Strong's policies, which Miller had criticized so roundly, were of course also in lieu of a gold standard. However, as noted previously, Strong always believed that a gold standard should and would be reinstituted when European banks again had enough gold to make the international gold standard practicable. By 1927 some European central banks had accomplished the beginning stages of such a return, and in 1928 Strong had made it very clear that he absolutely favored a return to a true gold standard.

Second, no Fed authority, and no economist except Warburton (in the 1960s), mentioned the Board's prescriptive power to set aside all gold reserve requirements—for 30 days, to begin with, and with the additional authority to renew such suspensions every 15 days thereafter for an indefinite period (Board of Governors 1961: 34–35).[4] Indeed, this is the provision that allowed Fed banks to be considered effective lenders of last resort.

Third, the Fed Board violated all five of Walter Bagehot's rules for a central bank operating under the rubric of the gold standard. The rules were (1) lend freely, (2) lend at "high" (penalty) interest rates, (3) lend on bank paper that would be good when conditions were normal, (4) advertise this policy boldly, and (5) "carry on" until all the banks' gold reserves are gone. Miller and the other real bills advocates in power paid no attention to these precepts. They did not mention them and might have had no knowledge of them.

Fourth, the gold reserves of approximately $3.58 billion (5,900 tons) accounted in the Fed banks' "Consolidated Statement of Condition" were not used in any systematic or meaningful way—or even mentioned—during the contraction. This amount of gold was

---

[4] This provision also included an interest rate penalty on the Fed banks that violated the gold reserve requirement.

far more than enough to have promoted a recovery and a Strong-type price level stabilization policy. With the gold reserve requirement legally suspended, the Fed banks could have used all of their gold to satisfy any panic demands for reserves. Financial conditions, however, never would have reached such a pass in a Strong-led system, and emergency leniency for gold reserve requirements never would have been necessary (see Bordo, Choudhri, and Schwartz 2002).[5]

Fifth, the Fed's manifest policy failure was a major factor in stimulating doctrinaire Keynesianism, which fundamentally argued that no monetary policy in a free-market enterprise system could thwart less-than-full employment and economic stagnation. It was instrumental in promoting the idea that "money doesn't matter" and thereby retarded valid thinking in monetary theory for about 20 years—until the studies of Arthur C. Pigou (1951) and Don Patinkin (1951) on the real balance effect and the automaticity of "full employment."

Just as Benjamin Strong had altered the gold standard Federal Reserve System of 1913 to become a quantity theory Federal Reserve System in 1922, so Adolph Miller and a bare majority of the Fed Board converted Strong's version into a Real Bills Federal Reserve System in 1929. But while Strong's institution successfully managed a stable price level—and stated its intention of returning the Fed to a gold standard system—Miller's institution provoked an ongoing disequilibrium that continued for four years and then required another eight years for its exhaustion (see Miller 1935b).[6]

Since most banks could not get help from Fed banks after 1930 because of the quarantine on speculative "credit," commercial banks were failing by the hundreds—and still with no gold standard. With their demise, depositors saw their checkbook balances disappear. Depositors' defense against this unhappy—but now anticipated—event was to convert their bank demand deposits into currency. They wrote checks for "cash" to themselves, which reduced their deposit balances

[5] See Table 1 for a summary of how all the monetary variables suffered during this period while monetary gold increased.

[6] Miller noted that the Fed Board discontinued the "direct pressure" policy in June 1930, a year and a half after it was initiated.

at banks and gave them hand-to-hand currency—Federal Reserve notes, silver certificates, gold certificates, or national banknotes. However, all of these currencies made up the bank reserves that had supported their demand deposit balances, which had been a multiple of the currency reserves that they had just stashed in their business safes and household cookie jars. Yes, the nonbank public now had more currency, which was safe from bank failures, but the banks' reserves that had supported multiple dollars of checkbook balances were gone and the bank deposits with them (see Table 2). Real holdings of hand-to-hand currency almost doubled, while real values for checking accounts were almost halved between 1930 and 1933.

Ironically, the policy of direct pressure violated the positive dimension of the Real Bills Doctrine, for it trumped lending to needy but speculatively tainted banks that actually had "real bills" to discount. It thereby aggravated the very condition that the Federal Reserve Act

TABLE 2

Nominal and Real Components of the Money Stock, 1925–1934

	ALL COMMERCIAL BANK DEPOSITS PLUS CURRENCY OUTSIDE BANKS M(2)		DEMAND DEPOSITS D(D)		CURRENCY OUTSIDE BANKS (C)		TIME DEPOSITS T(D)	
YEAR	$	REAL	$	REAL	$	REAL	$	REAL
1925	100	100	100	100	100	100	100	100
1926	105	104	103	102	101	100	107	106
1927	108	109	103	104	100	100	114	115
1928	113	115	104	108	101	103	123	125
1929	114	115	105	107	102	103	123	125
1930	113	118	101	106	94	99	125	132
1931	109	125	93	106	102	117	125	144
1932	94	119	73	93	129	165	107	137
1933	85	115	67	92	133	181	94	138
1934	92	119	78	102	131	170	99	129

Sources: Board of Governors (1943: 34, 35, 368). Real values derived using the Bureau of Labor Statistics' Consumer Price Index, 1935–1939 = 100, and using 1925 as the base year for Table 2.

was supposed to alleviate. Rather than basing loans and discounts on the merits of the paper offered for discount, as Miller had remarked in his testimony, direct pressure attempted to control the behavior of the member banks, not the credit they might grant. By the time the Fed Board desisted, the financial system was virtually destroyed.[7] George Norris, governor (i.e., president) of the Philadelphia Fed wrote as follows:

> This whole process of "direct action" is wearing, friction producing, and futile. We are following it honestly and energetically, but it is manifest beyond the peradventure of a doubt, that it will never get us anywhere. . . . Our 5 percent [discount rate] is equivalent to hanging a sign over our door "Come In" and then we have to stand in the doorway and shout "Keep Out." It puts us in an absurd and impossible position.[8]

---

[7] For many of the details on the substance of Federal Reserve policies, and the personalities behind them, see Meltzer (2003: 181–252).

[8] Memo from Norris to Fed Governor Charles Hamlin. Quoted in Chandler (1958: 467–68).

9

ECONOMISTS' VIEWS OF FED
MONETARY POLICIES, 1932–1933

At this point in the narrative, an important question arises: What did economists and political scientists think of the devastated banking system and unusually depressed economy that appeared beginning in 1930? What were their opinions on its causes? What did they think about the gold standard? Finally, what were their solutions to this overwhelming crisis? This chapter reviews those opinions and possible solutions.

The ongoing deflationary disequilibrium that extended from 1929 into early 1932 prompted the well-regarded political scientist Quincy Wright at the University of Chicago to initiate a "series of lectures that discussed the economic depression from both theoretical and practical points of view." Five prominent economists from prestigious universities, who presumably reflected various schools of monetary thought, gave papers that were published as a book, *Gold and Monetary Stabilization*. The book, edited by Wright ([1932] 1983), also included an appendix: "Recommendations of Twenty-Four Economists Present at the Institute." The economists' papers and subsequent recommendations were supposed to reflect their opinions on the gold standard— whether it was working as it was supposed to, what role the Federal Reserve System should or could have within the framework of that standard, and what other policies might be desirable.

The first paper at the Chicago conference, "International Aspects of the Gold Standard," was read by Jacob Viner, who at the time was a professor of economics at the University of Chicago. Viner complained that "much of the great increase in bank credit [during the 1920s] . . . went into security and real estate speculation instead of into commerce." He deplored "the anarchic way in which the gold standard has been operating," and labeled it "a wretched standard . . . but it may conceivably be the best available to us." He noted further that "U.S. gold reserves are still . . . far in excess of our minimum needs. . . . With minor changes in our legal gold reserve requirements, we could stabilize prices without imperiling our continued adherence to the gold standard. . . . The gold standard," he concluded, "has rightly been put on the defensive, and only substantial assurance of better performance in the future than in the past will entitle it to a new lease on life" (Wright [1932] 1983: 20, 25, 37–39).

Viner's remarks showed that he barely understood or tolerated what he thought was "the" gold standard. He was apparently unaware that the operational gold standard had been severely compromised by wartime pressures, by Strong's stable price level policy from 1922 to 1929, and especially by the Fed Board's real bills–inspired anti-speculation policy from 1929 to the time of the conference in early 1932. His paper was mistaken on historical facts and otherwise shallow and unproductive.

Gottfried Haberler of Harvard University gave the second paper, "Money and the Business Cycle." Where Viner had demonstrated at least superficial observation and analysis of current events, Haberler discussed virtually none of the current monetary problems—the gold standard, gold policies, central banking policies—nor any monetary data. His lecture reflected only his interest in the theory of business cycles; it had little or nothing to do with the current economic disequilibrium.

THE REAL BILLS PERSPECTIVE

H. Parker Willis gave the third lecture, "Federal Reserve Policy in Depression," and his 30-page paper was very revealing. Willis, as noted earlier, was one of the all-time principal real bills advocates, a student and close friend of J. Laurence Laughlin, an adviser on the development of the Federal Reserve Act, and a close associate of Adolph Miller. His lengthy paper reflected the confusion that the institutional mixture of the era—gold standard, Federal Reserve

System, Real Bills Doctrine, and quantity theory of money—had provoked. It also reflected much of the book on the Fed that he had published in 1915 (see Willis 1915).

In his lecture Willis called "attention, first of all, to the general question of what a central bank is, and what it should, or can do, on any occasion." "Fundamentally," he explained, "a central bank is an institution vested . . . with public duties." He denied that it was a "bankers' bank," or that it should "afford relief to hard-pressed banks, as is often alleged." "A central bank," he continued, "is a public or people's bank" that operates without regard to profit. Its functions are "to hold safely the ultimate reserves of the country, [and] to ascertain the national need for specie reserve and make sure that it is adequately provided." The central bank was also the system's clearinghouse and should supply "available liquidating power" wherever reserve funds were most needed. He regarded the Fed banks as part of the commercial banking system, not as separate institutions exercising controls over it. Both banks and central banks, he emphasized, should follow "the many canons of banking soundness that [are] regarded as almost sacred"— that is, the "canons" of the Real Bills Doctrine (Wright [1932] 1983: 82–84). Nevertheless, since the "people's bank" held the gold reserves for the whole banking system, it had to have a theory or program on how to manage such reserves. It could not hold all that gold and have no principles for its use.

To show what had gone wrong with the system, Willis quoted at length from Benjamin Strong's memorandum on the policy of the New York Fed during the minor recession of 1924. That episode, Willis stated, "was the best exposition of the point of view by which the policy of the system has been, and is, controlled" (86–92). Later, describing the situation after 1929, Willis continued in an astonishingly disingenuous passage:

> There was a descending trend in the price level, and a general disposition on the part of most persons in the stock market to abstain from active dealings in shares. There was no demand for "money,"

because no one wanted money on loan. There was a general desire to get "funds" through the processes of liquidation, but there was no disposition to borrow for the purpose of carrying stocks or securities at the inflated prices that then still existed. (93)[1]

Willis's disquisition made it seem as though all these actions and inactions were normal market happenings, rather than results of the Federal Reserve's policy of direct pressure, which he did not mention.

In his summary, Willis emphasized Strong's stable price level policy when the New York Fed controlled policy in the 1920s. His account implied that the Real Bills Doctrine replaced the quantity theory of money as a guiding principle of monetary policy in 1929. However, he did not mention his friend and colleague, Adolph C. Miller, who had come into power in 1929 together with other real bills proponents and instituted the direct pressure policy that virtually froze Fed bank lending. Rather, according to Willis, after 1929 "there was no demand for money" and a downward "trend" in the price level.

Of course, banks and everyone who was being liquidated wanted "funds," which they were getting by a fire-sale liquidation of assets. The export of gold, Willis continued, suddenly became an issue when Britain went off the gold standard in 1931. But the Fed Board and banks raised interest rates and the "outward movement of gold [from the United States] ceased, although the higher rates of the Reserve banks had no effect in changing or reducing the amount of demand for any type of loanable funds." Banks had been failing on an "enormous and unprecedented scale," and the business public had found it "at times impossible to get loans on any terms." He continued that the Fed banks, being unable to deal directly with individuals and business enterprises, were for that reason ineffectual. He raised the question of "how far any federal reserve system . . . can remedy or relieve depression, or . . . hold in check tendencies to higher prices . . . than otherwise would be undertaken"—no quantity theory of money here!

---

[1] Stock market prices may have been "inflated," but the rest of the U.S. economy's price structure was eminently stable. Willis was here continuing the mistaken notion that inflated stock market prices spelled "inflation" for the entire market economy.

He found it "strange" that within recent weeks there had been a revival "of the 'cheap money' policy [stable price level policy of the 1920s], and yet such is the case" (95).

The ongoing depression, Willis observed, had demonstrated the fundamental flaw in the Federal Reserve System:

> Reserve banks are bankers' banks which deal only with member institutions or, more truly stated, are stock market banks, which have so restricted their own field of operations that they cannot reach the rank and file of business institutions even if they would, but must work through the market. . . . The Federal Reserve banks have found themselves confined to the comparatively limited group of institutions which deal in government bonds . . . and in bankers' acceptances, and [the System] has refrained from even exercising the open market powers which were given to it for direct dealing in commercial paper. . . . Summing up the actual results, then, of Federal Reserve policy in depression, we must conclude that they have been very largely theoretical, [except that they have caused] the redistribution of gold reserve [to foreign countries]. . . . We must [also] conclude that Federal Reserve policy in time of depression will always be more or less ineffectual. . . . The best Federal Reserve policy will be that of "hands-off" with [rediscount] rates maintained at a normal level. . . . [All attempts to] place funds in the stock market . . . are likely to cause trouble, [to] aggravate dangers already existing, and hence to be a harm rather than a relief. (96–100)

After this distortion of reality—although he seemed to believe it—Willis raised the fundamental question of what the underlying basis for central bank policy, and particularly for the Federal Reserve System, ought to be. He repeated this question for emphasis: How far can any central banking system, including the Fed, "remedy or relieve depression, or conversely prevent higher prices than would otherwise occur?" He distinguished between commercial banking policy, within which he included central bank policy, and "the natural current of events in business." When "credit" is extended by a reserve bank through open market operations for long-term paper, he explained, recipients get "short-term funds [bank credit] . . . available for any use they choose." This action will only be wise if the funds have an "economic use":

> Any such step at the present time [early 1932] would simply mean an aggravation of existing difficulties, due to the fact that we are already overburdened with construction work and fixed capital that are not soon likely to be employed. The funds may also go into the hands of bankers . . . to meet the demands of depositors, but it is doubtful that they have any more permanent effect. (105)

Here Willis listed the following "dangers . . . produced by such artificial releases of credit" (105–6):

- "Placement of funds in the hands of persons who . . . have not asked for and do not need them"
- Creation of new liabilities on the part of central banks, which they must keep convertible into gold
- Consequent danger of inability to maintain gold redemption
- Prospect that this new "credit" might do more harm than good by being used "where it is not needed"[2]

Willis believed that "a central bank is a dangerous agency through which to undertake inflation, the more so when we remember that its operations may easily get out of hand and prove disastrous." He noted that the policies under Strong, which he had earlier quoted, were of this "hazardous" and "unsuccessful" nature (106–7).

Willis concluded by emphasizing that the question of policy, whether current or long range, was a "basic issue about which some positive and final conclusion must be reached before we can manage our banking system soundly." He noted that only two countries

---

[2] By this time, professional sentiment favoring Federal Reserve open-market operations to revive total spending had obtained much professional favor.

[the United States and France] had been able "to maintain the gold standard in theoretically full working order" (107).[3]

If Miller's damning of speculation and his punishing policy of direct pressure initiated the beginning and ongoing nightmare of the Great Contraction, Willis's discussion three years later was a confirmation. Although Willis did not mention either Miller or direct pressure, he undoubtedly knew and approved of the Fed Board's actions. He simply pretended that the wholesale bank failures were a natural outcome of errors by commercial bank managers. His entire discussion in the last 15 pages of his 30-page paper reflected the real bills philosophy: production brings forth the money to finance it, and any positive policy by a central bank that tries to supply money where it is not known to be "needed" is ill advised.

The Real Bills Doctrine owed its initiation to a freely working gold standard. However, a Real Bills Doctrine that supplants a gold standard, and dominates monetary policy under the rubric of gold, is far from stable. While the gold standard was dominant and the Real Bills Doctrine just another proper principle for sound banking, the doctrine was benign. But when the anti-speculative element of the doctrine became the guiding principle for Fed policies in 1929, taking the initiative away from the functioning gold standard, it provoked a cataclysmic disaster in both the monetary system and the real sector.

THE CASE FOR THE TRADITIONAL GOLD STANDARD

The fourth paper of the Chicago conference, "The Future of the Gold Standard," by Lionel D. Edie, an economist with the Investment Research Corporation and a former professor of finance at the University of Chicago, accurately described the gold standard and the impediments Fed policy had introduced to its functioning. Edie first discussed the Bank of England's abandonment of gold parity in September 1931, the event that had prompted the conference. He noted that the United States still had over $4 billion of gold, an

---

[3] All that Willis's statement could mean was that gold payments for common money were still happening, but "the" gold standard was not functioning in a Real Bills mode. By "theoretical" he only meant that central bankers were following gold reserve ratios in their management of national currencies.

amount that "would be ample to support the functioning of the Federal Reserve System." However, he added, "The hoarding of [hand-to-hand] currency has given rise to alarm . . . due to the provisions of Federal Reserve note issue. . . . When collateral is limited additional [Fed] note issue by banks must be backed practically 100 per cent by gold" (Edie [1932] 1983: 114).

Edie here referred to the original Federal Reserve Act, which required Federal Reserve notes to be backed 40 percent by gold, while the remaining 60 percent could be secured by "eligible paper," that is, real bills. However, if no real bills were "available," the issue of notes had to be collateralized 100 percent by gold. Nothing "speculative," such as stock market assets, or anything long-term or "unproductive," such as government securities or mortgages, were legal collateral.[4]

Edie gave an accurate précis of how gold under a gold standard regulated the money supply. "Due to its limited production," Edie explained, "the gold stock cannot be subject to violent fluctuations. This relative stability in gold supply over short periods commends gold highly as a monetary base. In brief, the primary economic function of the gold standard is a supply [of money] function. This supply function is to protect economic society from excessive short-term fluctuations in money" (118). Unfortunately, Edie continued:

> Something has gone wrong in the machinery for relating [bank] credit to gold . . . with the result that . . . the gold base does not hold the credit superstructure in line. *The Federal Reserve Act cut the tie which binds the gold reserve directly to the credit volume and by so doing automatically cut off the basic function of the gold standard.* . . . People talk about abandoning the gold standard, without realizing that in an essential respect we abandoned it some time ago. . . . We did so unintentionally and unconsciously, but effectively none the less. We are not now on the gold standard, in so far as its supply [of money] function is concerned, and we have not been for some time. True, we have the trappings,

---

[4] Shortly after this conference, Congress passed a law allowing government securities to be eligible collateral for Fed notes. However, this adjustment came much too late to retard the contraction.

earmarks, and accessories of the gold standard, but we do not
have the essential economic service of that standard because gold
has been divorced from [bank] credit. Member bank reserve balances [accounted in Federal Reserve Banks' balance sheets] are
the intermediary between gold and [commercial bank] credit.
These balances are the active base of our whole banking system.
(120; emphasis added)[5]

Edie cited several variables that caused undesirable fluctuations in
banks' reserve balances: currency flows from one section of the country
to another, gold imports and exports that effected changes in the Fed's
gold base, Fed bank rediscounts to member banks, [real] bills held by
Fed banks, and government bonds held by the Fed. "Fluctuations in
these items," Edie observed,

may occur at times and in amounts which exaggerate waves
of inflation or deflation and which make possible extremes of
speculation or liquidation. There is no saving grace inherent in
the situation which assures that these variables will give orderly
movement to the net reserve base. . . . Inasmuch as we are here
concerned with a period of excessive deflation, we may consider
that side of the picture only, but that is not to overlook danger of
converse excesses on the side of inflation. (121)[6]

Edie then discussed how the variables he cited acted to provoke
the low-level equilibrium of business activity at the time:

All of these considerations tend to produce a stalemate in central bank policy and to allow the irrational forces of liquidation
to proceed unimpeded. . . . [Then] these volatile and unstable
factors have the effect of cutting off the fluctuations of credit
from the moderating influence of the gold base. . . . [I]t is not

[5] Edie's statement here is an astounding revelation of facts that seems to have escaped the understanding of many other participants, including Viner. Nothing that followed indicated how the other
economists at the conference regarded Edie's enlightening analysis.

[6] For such an example, see the present volume's Chapter 5 on the German hyperinflation of 1922–1923.

an exaggeration to state that the United States has already abandoned the gold standard in the sense that it has abandoned the
supply function of gold as a regulator of the credit. . . . I sub-
mit that the real threat to the gold parity . . . is to be found in
the unstable factors which permit such an excessive contraction
of credit as has been witnessed in the United States during the
past two years [1929–1931]. . . . It is time to recognize that the
Federal Reserve mechanism does not constitute an automatic
self-corrective device for perpetuating the gold standard. On the
contrary, it contains within itself the seeds of its own destruction
unless a clearer conception of the responsibilities of central bank
leadership can be established. (126–28)

Edie's insight was profound. He is the only economist of this era,
besides Lauchlin Currie, who seems to have understood what Fed
policy was doing not only to the money supply but to the entire credit
structure.[7]

If the United States were willing to correct the flaw in the Federal Reserve mechanism by a definite plan for protecting the value of
the dollar from irrational excesses and deficiencies, he concluded, "the
world will hasten to return to a gold basis in which the dollar plays a
pivotal role" (129).

While Edie did not discuss the change in Federal Reserve leadership from Strong and his stable price level policy to Miller and his
real bills policy, his reasoning was all very accurate, as well as unique
for the time. Even then, he understood that the gold standard was
not functioning according to its traditional blueprint because Federal
Reserve policy had disrupted its natural workings.

Edie gets high marks for his insightful analysis. If the Chicago
conference had accepted his reasoning, the gold standard would have
been restored, Federal Reserve policy would have been revised, and
the Great Contraction reversed.

---

[7] For additional information on Lauchlin Currie see Chapter 13 of this volume.

THE PRAGMATIC CONVENTIONAL SOLUTION

The last paper presented at the Chicago conference was by John H. Williams of Harvard University. According to the director of the conference, Williams "was asked to contribute [an] article on the practical problems of relieving the depression, with special attention to [the] subject matter of the recommendations" to which conference participants had called attention (Wright [1932] 1983: x).

In his paper, "Monetary Conditions and the Gold Standard," Williams first noted the "implication . . . derived from the early [British] banking school, that business under these conditions creates and extinguishes its own 'legitimate' supply of credit"—that is, a real bills tendency to supply credit where it is needed and eliminate it when it is not needed. "In still another view, post-war [World War I] experience has shown that there is no middle ground between an automatic gold standard and a managed credit standard, and that the way out [of the dilemma] is a return to the automatic system [that is, to the gold standard]. . . . More numerous than any of these [theories] is the school which advocates monetary stabilization by central bank management"—by which Williams meant a stable price level policy of the type Strong had initiated (134–35).

Williams identified three policy alternatives: (1) adherence to a gold standard, (2) a stable price level policy, or (3) a policy centered on real bills. However, since 1922 the Fed had followed only the latter two: The gold standard had been in remission. "The boom of 1928–29," he added,

> took primarily the form of commercial loans for financial specu-
> lation.[8] The Reserve System met it with an attempt to discrimi-
> nate between loans for commercial and for speculative purposes.
> Its complete failure should explode once and for all the notion
> that it is possible to dictate the uses to which credit is put, rather
> than the quantity of credit for all purposes. (138)

---

[8] Williams offered no evidence in support of his use of "speculation."

Williams obviously understood the two disparate versions of policy that the Fed had adopted up to this time. He also understood, agreeing with Edie, that "in the strict theory of the gold standard there is no room or need for central bank control of credit. Control is achieved automatically by the flow of gold between [foreign and domestic] banking systems. . . . Credit expansion or contraction in one country is communicated by gold flow to other countries" (138).

The international gold flow system works best, Williams summarized, when institutions and prices respond according to the usual economic fundamentals—flexible prices, felicitous capital movements, and so forth. He reviewed with much detail how international trade, capital movements, and gold flows, particularly by the Bank of England, had stabilized international commerce in the past. In the present (that is, the early 1930s), however, "there is a fundamental conflict between the principles of central banking and the principles of the gold standard. . . . A surplus of free gold leaves room for play between gold flow, bank credit, and prices. . . . Central banks may offset the effects of gold flows by their open-market operations" (148).[9]

Williams then commented at length on how the gold standard could be thwarted by those who managed policy from their central banking control towers. With a central bank that could counteract the gold standard, "it seems clear not only that the gold standard cannot be operated under modern conditions upon its original principles but also that, however managed, it cannot serve as the sole criterion of credit policy. . . . The wonder is that the gold standard should have worked as well as long as it has done" (155).

Williams pursued this line of reasoning by arguing that "credit management" by a central bank is a necessary adjunct to a working gold standard. "[A] country like our own," he continued, "which has capacity for very wide variations in its supply of purchasing power well within the limits set by its gold reserves, is compelled to find other criteria for the management of credit" (155). This last observation was a "criticism" of the gold standard only because a Federal Reserve policy

[9] Here Williams is confused by what a central bank makes possible and what a central bank—the Fed—was actually doing.

was in place that had already violated the course of policy a gold standard would have provided. It did not offer a reason for any alteration of the gold standard itself.

Williams seemed not to be aware that the Federal Reserve Act, which established Fed banks with variable gold reserve ratios, was the reason that a central bank was necessary for "credit management." In other words: no Federal Reserve Act, and no Fed banks with fractional gold reserves, then no necessity for credit management. Nevertheless, he concluded, "[T]he world will undoubtedly return to [a gold standard] in some form or other, even though eventually it may be outgrown" (155–57).[10]

Williams offered the obvious pragmatic conclusion: "The immediate problem is to restore normal conditions. The greatest single help, internally, would be a vigorous open market policy [of government securities] designed to reduce rediscounts of member banks and to increase the supply of purchasing power" (157).[11]

RECOMMENDATIONS STEMMING FROM THE CHICAGO CONFERENCE

The final exercise of the conference managers was to compile and forward to President Herbert Hoover a list of recommendations that the conference attendees had adopted. The recommendations were as follows:

- "We recommend that the Federal Reserve banks give a substantial preference in discount rates to commercial paper eligible as cover for Federal Reserve notes. . . . We recommend these measures as an effective means of increasing the free gold of the Federal Reserve System and as constituting an important defense against the consequence of gold withdrawals. We regard these measures as necessary prerequisites for the following recommendation with respect to open-market operations." (In February 1932, Congress passed the Glass-Steagall Act that provided for these changes.)

[10] As this analysis confirmed, the only gold standard that works like a gold standard should work is one not linked in any way to a central bank.

[11] That is, abandon the gold standard and follow a Benjamin Strong policy of price level stability.

- "We recommend that the Federal Reserve banks systematically pursue open-market operations with the double aim of facilitating necessary government financing and increasing the liquidity of the banking structure"—that is, a "Benjamin Strong" policy.

- "We urge that the Reconstruction Finance Corporation . . . carry out those provisions of the Act which authorize it to give aid to banks by making loans on assets not eligible for rediscount with Federal Reserve Banks"—that is, on loans that were not based on real bills.

- "We recommend that the federal government maintain its program of public works and public services."

- The next recommendation called for scaling down or canceling "intergovernmental debts" left over from World War I. The burden of these debts had increased significantly in real terms.

- The last recommendation called for negotiations with other countries to lower tariffs. (Wright [1932] 1983: 161–63)

The conference made no recommendations pertaining to the gold standard.

This list of recommendations was signed by 24 of the professional economists present, 12 of whom were employed at the University of Chicago. Most of those who signed were well known in their profession. Three who did not sign, but who had taken a significant part in the proceedings by reading papers, were Gottfried Haberler, H. Parker Willis, and Lionel D. Edie. No explanation was given for why these conference participants did not sign the list of recommendations (161).[12] Undoubtedly, Willis did not approve of open market operations in government securities; Edie may have felt that the recommendations dealt inadequately with restoration of the gold standard and a correction of Federal Reserve policy. Haberler probably thought that since there was no "business cycle" showing, his opinion was inconsequential.

---

[12] The conference report did not include any special remarks by the participating economists.

10

VIEWS ON MONETARY POLICY AFTER THE CHICAGO CONFERENCE

The economists' recommendations from the Chicago conference in late January 1932 had only a limited impact on Federal Reserve policymakers, congressional opinions, or policies that would have countered the ongoing depression. Nonetheless, several representatives as well as some officers in the Reserve System, sensing that Federal Reserve anti-speculation policies were adversely affecting monetary and business conditions, had begun a movement to add money to the economy by some means or other. In Congress, a bill was under consideration that would have ordered the Fed to issue $3 billion of Federal Reserve notes. The bill became known as the "Thomas Amendment." Some Federal Reserve governors, and Fed Board members as well, were of the same mind.

Accordingly, beginning in February 1932—just after the Chicago conference—the Federal Open Market Investment Committee began a very modest program of purchasing government securities. Secretary of the Treasury Ogden Mills, who was also ex officio chair of the Fed Board, had long been in favor of such an action. On February 13, 1932, he exclaimed: "For a great central banking system to stand by with a 70 percent gold reserve [against its monetary obligation] without taking active steps in such a situation [is] almost inconceivable. . . . The resources of the System should be put to work on a scale commensurate with the existing emergency" (Friedman and Schwartz 1963: 385).[1]

Through the spring of 1932 the security purchase program continued, but as Friedman and Schwartz (1963) document, it was constantly vitiated by real bills governors of some Fed banks and by the

[1] It is not certain that Mills had read the conference recommendations, but they were publicized enough that he may have.

real bills members of the Fed Board. Many economists and other observers thought by this time that recovery was at hand. However, by the end of June 1932 the net addition to the monetary base "was only $100 million in Federal Reserve credit," a pittance in terms of what was needed. After August 10, 1932, the security purchase program became moribund; no further increases were made to the monetary base. A latter-day recession then became superimposed on the depression that, had the proper reflationary policies been followed, should have ended (Friedman and Schwartz 1963: 389).

CHARLES O. HARDY

Also in 1932, the Institute of Economics at the Brookings Institute published a book, *Credit Policies of the Federal Reserve System*, by Charles O. Hardy, an economist on the Brookings staff. Hardy had attended the Chicago conference as a representative of Brookings, and his book treated many of the same issues that the economists at the conference had discussed. He also signed the petition that called for an expansive open market policy. Although Hardy's book was published in August, some months after the conference ended, he had been working on the substance of it for much longer.[2]

Hardy began by reviewing the high level of business activity in the 1920s and the financial boom of late 1927 and into 1928. In February 1929, Hardy (1932: 51) wrote: "There was instituted a new policy of 'direct pressure,' that is, refusal to lend to banks which were making call loans on stock market security. . . . During March and April [1929] indications were that the Board had been measurably successful in securing the cooperation of member banks . . . to cut down the proportion of credit which was being used for security speculation." Hardy's observation on "securing cooperation" was surely a euphemism. The direct pressure policy on the member banks was obligatory.

Hardy then discussed at length the issue of how the Federal Reserve System dealt "with the problem of control of speculation."

---

[2] According to an offhand note in the book itself, Hardy had finished writing it in June 1932, but he could not have written such a book in less than one year. No doubt he thought that the Chicago conference's recommendations would be implemented.

He cited Federal Reserve reports and other documents to show that, from 1919 on, the Fed Board frequently censored speculation, while the Fed Bank of New York under Strong's influence argued that "the only way it is practicable to exert any important influence over the credit situation is by direct or indirect control of the volume of reserve available as a basis for member bank credit . . . and that it cannot discriminate between applicants for bank credit, so long as these applicants present eligible paper." The other view, Hardy wrote, argued that the reserve banks

> look back at the collateral offered by the prospective borrower and take cognizance of the purpose for which the borrower proposes to use the funds, discriminating against speculative and in favor of "productive" demands. The first of these views is associated with the name of Governor Benjamin String . . . and the latter with that of Adolph C. Miller of the Federal Reserve Board. (Hardy 1932: 24)

Strong's realistic account of how member bank borrowing had to be objective—that is, without regard to the purpose of the loan—is in stark contrast to the pious edicts of Adolph Miller, but Hardy did not compare the two. Instead, he kept on about speculation: "If the main purpose [of the 1929 policy] was to check the growth of speculative activity, both the experiment of direct action and the use of credit restriction must be acknowledged failures. . . . There is no real reason to believe that Federal Reserve policy played a significant part in bringing about the decline" (140–41). But, he concluded, the discount rate and open market policies of 1928 and the direct pressure of 1929 "kept down the total amount [of credit] available for all uses" (144). One might add, "Yes, even legitimate uses."

Hardy also treated at length the policy of price level stabilization. He cited Gustav Cassel of Sweden who, Hardy wrote, "contends that the maintenance of a stable price level is the sole duty of central banks." Proponents for the first price stabilization bill introduced by Rep. James Strong in 1926, Hardy noted, included many well-known economists, such as Cassel, Irving Fisher, John R. Commons, Wilford I. King, and many more. "The opponents," Hardy wrote, "were chiefly officials of the Federal Reserve System, and included Adolph C. Miller of the Federal Reserve Board, Governor Benjamin Strong, Walter Stewart, and E. A. Goldenweiser of the System's Division of Research and Statistics" (205).

Hardy did not distinguish here between Governor Strong's case against the bill and that of Adolph Miller. Strong was, of course, a firm devotee of the quantity theory of money and a policy of price stabilization, but he did not favor putting it formally into law. Miller, on the other hand, denied both the quantity theory and, particularly, any effort by the Federal Reserve System to maintain whatever price stability might be possible.

The opponents of a policy of price stabilization, Hardy noted, argued that no price index was adequate. A stable price level bill, he observed, "would also rule out other tests of great importance." Stock prices and the condition of the money market also required the discretion of policymakers. Hardy denied that prices were necessarily stable from 1922 to 1929, because *some* indexes of *some* commodities showed *some* variation (210–11). He also noted that technological improvements in the qualities of goods are so profound over time that they change the nature of the goods and services to be priced (203). This observation is certainly realistic. Quality changes are very important and can seldom be priced. However, this problem can be treated by rebasing the price index every 10 years or so.

Hardy also understood that price stabilization was "incompatible with the maintenance of the gold standard. . . . No country could hold its own price [level] stable in the face of a worldwide change in the value of gold, and at the same time keep its currency freely interchangeable with gold in the world's markets at a fixed ratio" (222). This observation is entirely correct and is the main reason that Benjamin Strong objected to price stabilization as a *permanent* policy (207).

Hardy included an illustration of three different price indexes—a wholesale price index, a cost-of-living index, and the New York Fed's index of general prices—to show how variable price indexes can be for the same time period. These indexes, however, were consistently stable between 1922 and 1929 (210).

His analysis of the banking and Federal Reserve systems, Hardy wrote, "has made it clear that my own conclusions as to the merits of [price level] stabilization are unfavorable" (219). What kind of doctrinal Federal Reserve policy he *did* favor is not clear.

All the arguments, Hardy's included—however valid they might be about the nuanced differences among price indexes—really are beside the point. What is wanted is not a balancing of benefits for one special interest group or another, but some means of fixing the real value of the unit of account. Any scientifically constructed (weighted) index that samples all commodities and services, whether it includes everything or not, is a good-enough reflector of the value of money to serve the purpose of a price stabilization policy. Interestingly, the gold standard, when left undisturbed, very closely approximated this ideal. It did not favor any special groups, and it constrained prices—whether perfectly or not. A central bank keeping a price index constant could achieve a similar result.

In May 1932, Hardy noted, the House of Representatives passed the Goldsborough bill that would have had the Federal Reserve restore and maintain the average purchasing power of the dollar covering the years 1921–1929 "by the control of the volume of credit [bank deposits] and currency." Hardy added, "It establishes for the immediate future a price-raising policy; and for the long run a price-stabilization policy" (225). He did not expressly disapprove this policy, even though it included a stable price level provision.

Hardy could have been one of the principal speakers at the Chicago conference. His book reflected an in-depth knowledge of what was going on in the financial system. He did not, however, realize the fundamental importance of Benjamin Strong's stable price level policy between 1922 and 1930. And while he had a good understanding of Adolph Miller's policy of direct pressure after 1929, he nowhere indicated any appreciation of the link between that policy and the banking debacles that followed. His ignorance may be explained in part by timing: he was putting his book together before the final death throes of the commercial banking system in late 1932 and into 1933. Along with many other economists, he probably felt that recovery was imminent.

KARL R. BOPP

Some months after the Chicago conference, Karl R. Bopp wrote an article, "Two Notes on the Federal Reserve System," which was published in the *Journal of Political Economy* in June 1932. At the time he was an economics professor at the University of Missouri, and many years later he became president of the Federal Reserve Bank of Philadelphia. The timing of the article's publication meant that Bopp had written it some months after the January conference in Chicago; and though his article addressed some of the conference issues, Bopp did not refer to the findings and conclusions of that earlier event.[3]

The first "note" in Bopp's article was titled "The Absence of a Consistent Federal Reserve Policy." In particular, Bopp criticized the original Federal Reserve Act of 1913 for setting up not just one but several agencies within the system, ". . . which do have or are supposed to have some influence over policy." (Bopp 1932: 379) Besides the Fed Board, the act included the boards of directors of each Fed bank, a Federal Advisory Council, and a governor for each bank. In 1922 an open market policy conference added to the array.

The balance of power in this complex of forces, Bopp (1932: 379) noted, "is not merely a matter of law; it is also a matter of administration and personality. . . . Lack of consistency in policy is almost inevitable in the decisions of a Board whose membership changes [from time to time] and whose decisions are (in general) by majority vote." Many other practical variables had determined the course of policy action: "The Secretary of the Treasury was the dominant figure in the

---

[3] Bopp's article discussed two different subjects, thus the "Two Notes." Bopp was not at the 1932 Chicago conference. Jacob Viner, who was editor of the *Journal of Political Economy*, did attend the conference. Also at the conference and on the journal's editorial board was Lloyd W. Mints, who may have read and edited Bopp's article.

system during the World War, [while] Benjamin Strong, a governor, was for years the most important man in the system."[4]

Bopp cited three prominent economists of the era—Ralph G. Hawtrey, Gustav Cassel, and John Maynard Keynes—all of whom had written books in the 1920s in which they commented favorably on the stabilization of prices that Benjamin Strong had promoted in that era. By way of contrast, Bopp also quoted written opinions of the real bills proponents on the Fed Board—particularly Adolph Miller and Walter Stewart.

Price stabilization had been achieved prior to 1929. Since then, through 1931 and 1932, Bopp observed, Fed policy had been disparate and undefined. He cited several of Miller's published comments, which ranged from Miller's counter–price level stabilization comments in the 1920s to a final remark in January 1931, when Miller, testifying before a congressional committee, stated, "It was my opinion . . . in 1929 that the Federal Reserve System was drifting; that it was in a perilous situation without a policy." Bopp then editorialized, "If those at the helm are without rudder and compass, it is small wonder that the rest of us are waiting for ships that never come in" (Bopp 1932: 385).[5]

In his second note, "The Conflict of 1929 between the Federal Reserve Board and the Federal Reserve Bank of New York," Bopp treated the factors during World War I that had centered power in the Treasury Department. Strong, at that time governor of the Fed Bank of New York, had been instrumental in assisting Treasury policy. Continuing his analysis with the postwar period, Bopp noted that Strong had been the principal Fed official negotiating the loan made to the Bank of England in 1925. Bopp reported that Miller, a Board member throughout this period, "called the last occurrence 'a rather sorry and shabby episode'" (386). Presumably Miller felt this way because he and the rest of the Fed Board had not had any significant part in the proceedings.

---

[4] Bopp here noted the dichotomy (discussed in chaps. 5 and 6) between what we labeled the U.S. Treasury–Federal Reserve and the quantity theory–Federal Reserve.

[5] As seen earlier, Miller did not believe the "no-policy" assertion. He understood perfectly what Strong had done and was eager to change it. So by 1932 there had been two distinct policies.

The Board made efforts to increase its powers in 1929 after Strong had left the scene, Bopp noted. He did not mention Miller's direct pressure policy. But he did review the conflict between the Board and the Fed Bank of New York in 1929, especially with regard to the increase in discount rates to check the "speculative boom." Bopp wrote that he wanted to emphasize not the issue of whether a rate increase at that time was justified or not, but rather that "rivalry, jealousy, etc. may be more important in conditioning policy than are matters of high principle." The important argument that he chronicled, therefore, was not, as he had put it earlier, about "ships that never come in," but rather about the contrasting policies of the two helmsmen and their bureaucratic strength within the Fed—the Strong-led price stabilization policy starting in 1922, and the direct pressure policy from the Miller-led Board in 1929 and after. Bopp concluded his article with the following observation:

> It would appear . . . that the present [1932] dominant power within the Reserve system is the Federal Reserve Board. This [fact] means that our banking system is operating much like a central bank. One might favor such a system on general principles and yet regret (because of the personalities involved) that the change [to a central bank] came when it did. For example, statements by officials of the [regional] Reserve banks favoring an expansion of credit to stimulate revival lose much of their weight when not they but the Federal Reserve Board is in control. On the other hand, Mr. A. C. Miller, who seems to be the dominant figure on the Board, has stated that he is opposed to open-market operations—the only effective method of stimulating revival from a severe depression—except as a "surgical operation." Even through 1931 he was not of the opinion that such a "surgical operation" was necessary. (390)[6]

---

[6] By a "central bank" Bopp meant a regulatory system outside the commercial banking system. By way of contrast, Willis at the Chicago conference argued that the Fed was part of "the banking system" and not a regulatory agency acting on policy decisions.

Both the discussions at the Chicago conference and Bopp's paper in the *Journal of Political Economy* confirmed that Congress had not given the Federal Reserve System an unequivocal rule for initiating "credit" for the commercial banking system. Strong's policy from 1922 to 1929 had used a combination of measures to maintain price stability, while the real bills–inspired Miller policy thereafter had aimed primarily to counter stock market speculation. And the Fed, in the absence of specific legislation, had not developed any single-minded system of its own. Indeed, as Bopp implied, many observers did not regard it as a central bank at all. The Federal Reserve Act was ambivalent on who—if anyone—was to make important decisions or not make them.

LESTER CHANDLER'S TRIBUTE TO KARL BOPP IN 1970

Thirty-eight years after Bopp's article, another prominent economist, Lester V. Chandler, reviewed the Strong and Miller eras of the Fed. Chandler was a professor of economics at Princeton University, the author of a long-enduring textbook, *The Economics of Money and Banking* (New York: Harper and Row, 1948), and a professional friend of Karl Bopp. The year was 1970, and the occasion was Bopp's retirement as president of the Philadelphia Fed, a position he had achieved after his stint at the University of Missouri (Chandler 1970: 41–53).[7]

"How different the original Federal Reserve Act would have been," Chandler began in his speech,

> if it had been based on some sort of quantity theory of money, and how different might have been the speed, if not the direction, of evolution of Federal Reserve policies! The Act would undoubtedly have referred repeatedly to the supply of money and to regulation of its quantity in line with the needs of the economy for money balances. (42)

---

[7] Bopp taught at the University of Missouri from 1931 to 1941, when he joined the Philadelphia Fed.

However, the act was not based on a quantity theory of money, "but on a commercial loan theory of banking"—another common term for the Real Bills Doctrine.[8]

Chandler emphasized many of the points discussed earlier— H. Parker Willis's academic explanation of the doctrine, Sen. Carter Glass's long-time support in Congress, and official Fed emphasis on "credit" rather than the stock of money. He accurately recounted Strong's stable price level policy and how it had given way to the Miller policy of counterspeculation after 1929. "[T]he highly restrictive [anti-speculation] policies adopted to remedy the situation contributed far more to higher interest rates for 'legitimate' business than did any 'absorption of credit in the stock market,'" Chandler observed. Furthermore, "the money supply had already fallen more than 10 percent before the [gold standard] crisis impinged upon the United States [in 1931]. . . . [T]he freedom of Federal Reserve action was not in any way limited by considerations relating to its gold reserve or free gold position" (46).[9]

Chandler then listed a number of economists of the era who were on both sides of the Fed's restrictive real bills policy. One group favored relying on the quantity theory of money to set Fed policies, and the other included all the prominent real bills proponents. These latter economists, Chandler continued, made three arguments:

First, they claimed that "such a policy [of monetary expansion] would prolong the depression. . . . The preceding 'inflation' [of stock market prices], Strong's stable price level policy, and 'excessive expansion of credit' had to be purged from the system." Monetary expansion would only "prolong both the necessary process of liquidation and the depression."

Second, "it was healthful for the volume of credit to fall in response to a decline in the needs of trade reflecting a decline in business activity or price levels." That is, the "needs of trade" had declined, and monetary policy had to adapt to this real change.

---

[8] Chandler did not use this term anywhere in his paper, even though it had been coined 25 years earlier by Lloyd Mints.

[9] "Free gold" meant Fed banks' holdings of "excess" gold certificate reserves.

Third, the Federal Reserve "should conserve its own liquidity ... and this could be assured only by limiting its earning assets to short-term, self-liquidating paper conforming to the commercial loan theory."

Chandler then reported that as late as 1935, "a group of 69 [real bills] economists sent a memorandum to Congress urging that the supply of noncommercial paper eligible for discount "be further restricted, not enlarged." "It is the function of a central banking system," the memo declared, "to maintain at all times a liquid portfolio, since the system holds the ultimate reserves of the nation's banks" (48).

Chandler, in his considered criticisms of Fed policy, managed to neatly encapsulate our goal in writing this book:

> A full explanation of [that episode of theory and policy] would require an investigation of the entire intellectual social, political, and economic environment. . . . Why . . . did so many [economists and policymakers] adhere to the commercial loan [real bills] theory, with its implications of passive accommodation to private demands for commercial credit rather than to the quantity theory, which suggests more positive control? Yet the commercial loan theory did have profound effects on the Federal Reserve. It influenced the very structure of the System . . . [I]t influenced the thinking of professional economists and others outside, and thus the environment in which the System operated. . . . Nor can we be certain that this theory, with its remarkable ability to survive repeated refutations, is finally dead. (51)

Chandler's excellent review of the Great Depression era inexplicably omits at least five points:

1. He never used the term "Real Bills Doctrine," referring always to the "commercial credit theory of banking." As a professional economist who had been around for 50 or so years, why did he not use Mints's label? Had he not read Mints's thesis, *A History of Banking Theory*, published in 1945, in which the Real Bills Doctrine received its label and was discussed critically?

2. He never mentioned the Miller policy of "direct pressure" that began in 1929. Had he not read Warburton's account of that policy published in a collection of Warburton's work on monetary policy in 1966? Nor did he mention Miller's apologia in the *American Economic Review* of 1935, which we have noted was the key factor in the Great Contraction.

3. He never referred to Friedman and Schwartz's epic work on monetary history that had been in print for seven years when he wrote this tribute to Bopp.

4. He hardly mentioned the gold standard, which was supposed to determine the economy's money supply even in the 1930s, or the inherent dichotomy between the gold standard and the Real Bills Doctrine. If he had, he might have realized that the commercial loan theory of banking had usurped the controlling and stabilizing forces of the gold standard.

5. He also neglected Bopp's contribution to the monetary policy argument.

Yet, even with all these omissions, Chandler's observations of monetary policy are all well taken and verifiable with the primary sources and details on the history of the Real Bills Doctrine that we have presented here.

A LATER VIEW OF FED POLICY

The many commentaries on Fed policies and the gold standard recorded here emphasize that the Federal Reserve Act had subverted the gold standard and had not replaced it with any workable alternative. Even though Fed banks had to hold gold certificates in high ratios against the member bank reserves and Federal Reserve note currency they created, the very fact that Fed banks held gold only as a reserve against other base moneys meant that Fed policymakers could use other assets held by Fed banks to substitute for Fed banks' gold holdings in order to create more money. Most important, the very fact that an "independent" institution could manage its balance sheet to determine monetary policies that had previously been the sole province of the market-sensitive gold standard meant just what Lionel Edie had observed, at least twice, at the Chicago conference: "The" gold standard was gone, and "we" had abandoned it some time ago. In fact, it had not been an operational institution since 1913.

Friedman and Schwartz (1963: 299–420) emphasized this intra-system dichotomy. They examined in great detail many primary works analyzing the Great Contraction, including the bureaucracy in the Fed and the disparate views of professional economists and other observers, including Bopp, on the crisis that by 1932 had become calamitous. They noted that "the Board [after 1929] explained economic decline and then banking failures as occurring despite its own actions and as the product of forces over which it had no control." The financial collapse, they continued, resulted from the shift of power from the Strong-led Bank of New York to the Fed Board in Washington and other Fed banks. They concluded with this insightful observation:

> It is a sound general principle that great events have great origins, and hence something more than the characteristics of the specific persons or official agencies that happened to be in power is required to explain such a major event as the financial catastrophe in the United States from 1929 to 1933. (Friedman and Schwartz 1963: 419)

The "something more" that fills the void Friedman and Schwartz identify is the *anti-speculative aspect* of the Real Bills Doctrine and the hold it had, not only on economists of the era, but more important on the controlling contingent of policymaking officials in the Federal Reserve System. While Friedman and Schwartz analyze and discuss the doctrine accurately and extensively in their great work, they do not quite come to grips with its primary responsibility for the monetary mechanics of the Great Contraction. Of course they could not cover everything; they had to leave a few issues for other researchers, standing on their shoulders, to unravel.

11

GOLD RESERVE REQUIREMENTS, GOLD STOCKS, AND THE GOLD STANDARD

By late 1932, gold-based money and the gold standard that had endured in England and later in the United States for over 300 years, and then in other countries, was gone. It is a grim irony that the Real Bills Doctrine, which the working gold standard had sired, had become the dominant force in Federal Reserve management. By damning speculation in the stock market that might have been aided by commercial banks, the real bills Federal Reserve Board had so constricted bank credit that the banking industry was in shambles, and the economy was in the most disastrous depression imaginable.

Without question, however, the gold standard was completely innocent of having any responsibility for the Great Contraction. If the gold standard had remained the dominant monetary institution without a central bank to "help" it, no Great Contraction would have begun in 1929. Counterfactual history can never be conclusive. But we believe the international gold standard could very well have been reinstituted in 1929 after Strong's interim stable price level policy. If it had, and if the new exchange rate structure had been realistic,[1] no significant change in the price level, or in bank credit and the overall quantity of money, would have happened in 1929–1930. Subsequent adjustments under the authentic gold standard, without a dominating Real Bills Doctrine, would have been mild and market determined.

Perhaps the most astonishing residual of the Great Contraction and subsequent Great Depression is that almost all observers, both

---

[1] "Realistic" means that most countries' postwar mint prices for gold would have had to be increased—that is, the gold content of the mint units of account would have had to be reduced in accordance with the changes in price levels that by this time seemed permanent. The pound sterling, for example, would have been approximately in purchasing power equilibrium with the dollar if its parity value had been changed from $4.86+ to about $4.44.

at the time and then throughout the 20th century, have damned the gold standard as the offending institution. Reasoning only deductively, an observer might ask—as the authors of this book have—how could an institution that had provided such a stable monetary environment through the centuries suddenly become a financial wrecking ball that generated a decade-long worldwide depression?

Indeed, no *operational* gold standard could have wreaked such havoc (Friedman and Schwartz 1963: 474–75). What remains is to chronicle what happened to monetary gold, gold contracts, and the Federal Reserve as an agency of monetary policy *after* the Real Bills Doctrine had overrun the gold standard, upset the monetary apple cart, and so muddled the monetary system that no one could figure out what had happened, let alone what to do about it.

Recall that the Federal Reserve Act required Reserve banks to keep a minimum gold reserve of 40 percent against their issues of Federal Reserve note currency, plus a gold reserve of at least 35 percent against their holdings of reserve balances for member banks. The act specified no upper limit to the gold ratios prescribed for the banks; they could legally hold as high a percentage as they thought proper. In the event of an emergency, the act provided that the Federal Reserve Board could order the suspension ". . . of any [gold] reserve requirements specified in this Act" for a period of 30 days, and it could renew any such suspensions every 15 days thereafter for an indefinite period (Board of Governors 1961: 34–35).

Such an emergency policy, if followed, would have removed the Reserve Board from any position of gold management so that the authentic gold standard, by default, would have assumed its original character and reestablished monetary equilibrium by means of market forces. If the Fed banks somehow lost all their gold, they would simply have had to run with the wind like ordinary banks until conditions changed enough for domestic gold to flow back into the banks, or for gold from outside the U.S. banking system to come into the system through enhanced balances from international trade. The gold standard as a money-determining institution would again have been functioning, and a new market equilibrium would have appeared at a slightly lower price level. This stabilizing action occurred during the (slightly) depressed years, 1893–1896 (Timberlake 2007: 330–31).

What actually happened was quite different. Through 1931, gold "piled up" up in Fed banks or, to be more precise, in the Treasury. The gold was accounted in the Fed banks' balance sheets as gold certificates and was one of the two major assets in the "Consolidated Statement of Condition" of the 12 Fed banks.[2] By mid-1931 Fed banks had more than double the amount of legally required gold reserves (see Table 3). As late as March 1933, when the commercial banking system had been bled white and the economy was on the edge of chaos, Fed banks still had $1 billion of excess gold reserves and more total gold than they had had in 1929. This datum by itself makes clear that the gold standard was not operational.

During the years of the Great Contraction, Federal Reserve officials expressed great concern about the paucity of Fed banks' gold holdings—that is, the dollar value of their gold certificate assets. Their statements implied that Fed policies were very much constrained by the "limited" quantity of monetary gold held as reserves in Fed banks, as well as by the alleged scarcity of commercial paper eligible for discount.

On both counts, nothing was further from the truth. In early 1932 the Fed banks had record holdings of gold certificate reserves, and the commercial banks were still inundated with commercial paper (see Table 3). Had it not been for the Fed Board's continuing crusade against speculation, and then the depressed banking system that the Board's anti-speculative policies had provoked, this quantity of gold reserves would have been far more than enough to reconstitute the commercial banking system's reserve base so that the banks could have expanded the real bills loans, discounts, and deposits that proponents of the Real Bills Doctrine extolled (see Friedman and Schwartz 1963: 391–99).

[2] Originally, gold certificates were similar to ordinary currency, but they were in $100,000 denominations to be suitable for banks to hold as reserves and to expedite bank clearings. They were adorned with a portrait of Woodrow Wilson, the president who signed the Federal Reserve Act. Later, they became just accounting sheet entries since no individuals, or even banks, could use them as hand-to-hand currency.

TABLE 3

The Fed's Gold Reserves and Other Monetary Data, 1928-1938 (Monthly Averages of Daily Figures)

DATE (YEAR-MONTH)	MEMBER BANK RESERVES	FEDERAL RESERVE NOTE CIRCULATION	GOLD AND OTHER RESERVES OF THE FEDERAL RESERVE BANK (EXCESS)	GOLD AND OTHER RESERVES OF THE FEDERAL RESERVE BANK (TOTAL)	GOLD RESERVE RATIO (4 ÷ 1 + 2)
	(1)	(2)	(3)	(4)	(5)
1928 Feb	2.37	1.60	1.49	2.97	74.0
1928 Aug	2.27	1.65	1.27	2.75	69.0
1929 Feb	2.36	1.66	1.32	2.83	69.4
1929 Aug	2.32	1.83	1.56	3.12	74.2
1930 Feb	2.31	1.68	1.66	3.16	78.3
1930 Aug	2.39	1.35	1.71	3.10	81.7
1931 Feb	2.37	1.47	1.81	3.25	83.4
1931 Aug	2.35	1.88	1.97	3.62	81.4
1932 Feb	1.91	2.66	1.38	3.15	67.4
1932 Aug	2.07	2.85	1.02	2.91	58.2
1933 Feb	2.29	2.92	1.35	3.36	63.1
1933 Aug	2.37	3.00	1.71	3.82	68.1
1934 Feb	2.82	2.96	1.62	3.87	64.4
1934 Aug	4.05	3.11	2.44	5.20	70.0
1935 Feb	4.60	3.12	2.80	5.75	72.1
1935 Aug	5.23	3.33	3.36	6.63	74.8
1936 Feb	5.81	3.67	4.24	8.02	78.0
1936 Aug	6.18	4.00	4.57	8.54	79.2
1937 Feb	6.75	4.17	4.95	9.14	80.3
1937 Aug	6.70	4.24	4.91	9.15	79.6
1938 Feb	7.23	4.13	5.20	9.59	80.3
1938 Aug	8.12	4.15	6.14	11.03	82.4

Note: All values in billions of dollars except reserve ratios.
Source: Board of Governors of the Federal Reserve System, Banking and Monetary Statistics, 1943: Table 93, 347-49.

As it was, the excess gold reserves that continued to appear in Fed banks' balance sheets provided grist for the mills of influential anti–gold standard economists and policymakers who chafed under the gold standard's discipline. They could argue that the gold standard was not working because the gold (certificates) remained on Fed banks' balance sheets and did not give rise to additional loans and deposits in commercial banks. These critics seemingly could not understand that an all-but-unseen Fed Board, in its anti-speculative zeal—not to say ignorance—had virtually sterilized the Fed banks' accounted monetary gold. The gold standard through these experiences became the whipping boy for all the unpleasant events that had occurred, as well as all that would occur in the future. Only a few economists, such as Lionel Edie, could see behind the accounting veil and understand that Fed policymakers had virtually impounded the Fed bank's gold (certificate) reserves.[3]

To summarize the events during the Great Contraction, 1929 to mid-1933: the accounted money stock of hand-to-hand currency plus all demand, time, and savings deposits in commercial banks declined by 25 percent; the number of commercial banks decreased from about 23,000 to 14,000 (that is, 9,000 banks failed); the price level, as measured by the CPI (1926 = 100) declined 25 percent; unemployment increased to 24 percent of the workforce; and real GNP fell 30 percent.

In a liquidity crisis—or any other defined crisis—whether Fed banks had "excess" gold reserves should not have represented a limitation. According to Walter Bagehot's rules, and also as implied by the Federal Reserve Act, *all* of the Fed banks' gold reserves were expendable—both the "excess" gold reserves and the remaining "required" reserves—to redeem common money with gold. That is what a gold standard means and what it had, in fact, meant in earlier times.

By the time the bloodletting ended in March 1933, bankers were shell shocked. The institution that was supposed to provide them with liquidity had actually created a liquidity crisis—although very few bankers or economists knew it at the time. Rather than being the solution, the Fed had turned itself into the problem—one that no other agency could solve. It had become a real bills Federal Reserve System at a time when it should have continued as a quantity theory of money central bank, and no working gold standard was there to save it.

The gold standard was a venerable institution. Gold had been the unofficial standard in Britain since 1688. For over 300 years the British pound sterling had an almost constant gold value (see Jastram 1977: 190–221). In the United States, the Constitution of

---

[3] Edie, however, did not identify either the Real Bills Doctrine or its proponents, nor could he have been expected to do so at that stage of the real bills development.

1789, Article I, Section 8 states, "The Congress shall have power . . . To coin money, regulate the value thereof, and of foreign coin, and fix the standard value of weights and measures." Two pages later it adds, "Section 10: No state shall . . . coin money; emit bills of credit; [or] make any Thing but gold and silver coin a [legal] tender in payment of debts." Most understandably, the point of declaring gold (and silver) a necessary base for all money creation was to limit the total amount of common money that banks or governments could create. The gold-silver base was not absolutely fixed; it could grow at the same modest rates as the world's production of gold and silver. It therefore provided a limited potential for growth in common money to accommodate the growth in real product of the economies that based their monetary systems on it.[4]

Through the 19th century and into the 20th, the gold standard, though occasionally interrupted by adventurous fiscal experiences and devastating wars, always returned to its traditional constraining principle for determining the economy's stock of money. In the United States, it survived Civil War financing and was reaffirmed in the (Gold Standard) Currency Act of March 14, 1900, and again in the Federal Reserve Act itself, which stated, "Nothing in this act . . . shall be considered to repeal the [gold] parity provisions contained in an act approved March 14, 1900."[5]

Nonetheless, in spite of the gold standard's venerable longevity and its effective check on many facets of government intervention over the centuries, contrary fiscal and monetary experiences in the United States and Europe during the 1920s and 1930s—which took place behind the *façade* of a gold standard—left that standard both disgraced and expendable. Throughout the decades that followed, its tarnished reputation has endured, especially its alleged responsibility for the Great Contraction. It is now regarded as outmoded, unnecessarily costly, undesirable politically, and a waste of good gold metal. Its feature as an automatic and limiting determinant of the stock of money

---

[4] While both gold and silver were constitutional moneys in order to provide needed denominations, silver tended to provide "too much" money and eventually was degraded to a fractional coinage status. To simplify our exposition, we refer only to gold.

[5] *Congressional Record*, 63rd Cong., 2nd sess., p. 5106.

in market systems is ridiculed, and it has been universally abandoned. Modern macroeconomic model building, advocates presume, does the job of monetary stabilization better.

This state of affairs is aptly demonstrated in many contemporary books and articles. One such book, *Golden Fetters: The Gold Standard and the Great Depression, 1919–1939* by Barry Eichengreen (1992), makes this case.

> Over much of Europe, the Depression was regarded as a product of excessive credit creation on the part of central banks that had failed to abide by the rules of the gold standard. . . . Under the gold standard, a smooth deflation like that of 1873–93 was the normal response.[6] But the central banks had blocked the downward adjustment of prices in the 1920s. . . . The resultant liberal supplies of credit [by the Federal Reserve System] had fueled speculation in financial markets, raising asset prices to unsustainable heights and setting the stage for the collapse in autumn 1929. . . .[7] In this view, the Great Depression was the inevitable consequence of unrealistic policies pursued by central banks in preceding years. . . . It was better [in 1929] to allow excess liquidity to be purged and prices to fall to sustainable levels (Eichengreen 1992: 301).

Nowhere in his book does Eichengreen mention the Real Bills Doctrine and its effect on central bank policies; nor does he recognize, despite repeated uses of the term "central bank," that central banks were running the show in all gold-standard countries. Former Fed chair Ben Bernanke's 1993 review in the *Journal of Monetary Economics* exhibits the same failings. Both he and Eichengreen pick on what had become a favorite whipping boy—the gold standard.[8]

---

[6] The "smooth deflation" was a result of the paper money (greenback) Civil War inflation of 1862–1865 and the silver inflation that followed. Restoring gold standard rules established a price level equilibrium that endured until 1913.

[7] "Asset" (i.e., stock market) prices are only a small fraction of all prices. *All prices*—that is, the price level— were almost constant. The logical solution, therefore, was not to take *all prices* down as asset prices declined, but rather to keep them constant while *asset prices* fell to their proper level, no matter what that was.

[8] For further discussion of what the gold standard had been, what it was in the early 1930s, and its destiny, see White (2012: 278–300).

In his review Bernanke wrote:

> In this masterful new book, Barry Eichengreen . . . has marshalled a powerful indictment of the interwar gold standard, and of the political leaders and economic policymakers who allowed themselves to be bound by golden fetters while the world economy collapsed. . . . While he is generally cautious about proposing a mono-causal explanation . . . [he] casts the gold standard as a principal culprit [Bernanke 1993: 254].

Throughout his review, Bernanke expresses the common opinion that the Fed in 1931 was "forced either to abandon gold or to adopt extremely deflationary policies in order to defend [sic] the legal parity of gold and the dollar."

This grievous denunciation of the gold standard has continued right up to the present. In a recent blog post, a very thoughtful and well-read economist, David Glasner, collected many of the arguments of anti–gold standard economists into a lengthy review article. Glasner (2016) cites Eichengreen's work, *Golden Fetters*, as well as a blog written by Ben Bernanke when he was Fed chair, and the work of Stephen Cechetti and Kermit Schoenholtz—all severe critics of the gold standard.[9]

Glasner is not as adamant an anti–gold standard critic as most economists through the past century. Nonetheless, he, like all the others, sees the post–World War I "gold standard" as a collection of central banks with fractional gold reserves trying to outmaneuver each other to get more of the fixed stock of gold. According to this view, central banks sell securities, thereby raising interest rates, and avoid as much as possible any policy that would increase the stock of common money.[10] Yes, some of the central banks—the Bank of France and the Federal Reserve banks—were more grasping than the others, and the hallowed prewar parities of the postwar era were a major deterrent to

---

[9] Other critical studies and comments on the gold standard include Temin (1989, 1994) and Sumner (2016).

[10] Neither Glasner nor any of the other economists he cites mention the Real Bills Doctrine and especially the restrictive monetary effect it had on Federal Reserve policies in the United States.

a more expansive policy. However, all of the analyses that Glasner and the others document were and are largely irrelevant to the functioning of an authentic gold standard.

What none of the critics seems to understand or treat in any scientific way are the essential properties of a *true* gold standard. The gold in the central banks these critics discuss was not the gold of a gold standard. Rather, it was a commodity under the discretionary control of central bank managers. To be gold-standard gold, the gold must be market directed. As we pointed out in Chapter 1, gold-backed money in a market environment appears in all markets and its disposition reflects market forces—the demand for gold-backed money relative to the utilities of common commodities, services, and capital.[11]

Even if the Fed, and other central banks in the 1930s, had done nothing more than follow Bagehot's principles and discounted good commercial paper—that is, real bills—tellingly and systematically, they would have restored the "normal" conditions that everyone desired. Even in the worst case, with the Federal Reserve banks' gold reserves exhausted—almost an impossibility—the commercial banking system would have been on a Federal Reserve note standard with a market price of gold slightly higher than the mint price. Gold from both internal and external sources, and a minor reduction in prices, would then have restored gold dollar parity in short order. A monetary system that succumbs to such a gold epidemic while fighting a rear-guard action, even though it never happened in the United States, is much more respectable than one that ends up with thousands of tons of gold reserves in the presence of a wrecked economy. A proper central bank does not fail if it loses all its gold reserves in a banking crisis. But, as Bagehot suggested, it may well fail if it does not.

[11] An exception to the negative gold standard literature is White (2016), who wrote:
Under a gold standard with competitive plural note-issuers (a free banking system) holding their own reserves, by contrast, the operation of the monetary system is governed by impersonal market forces rather than by any single agent. This is an important distinction between the properties of a gold standard with free banking and the properties of a gold standard managed by a central bank. The distinction is especially important when it comes to judging whether historical monetary crises and depressions can be accurately described as instances where "the gold standard failed" or instead where "central bank management of the monetary system failed."

12

THE WAR ON GOLD

The criticisms of the gold standard that appeared in the 1930s and thereafter were ubiquitous and vengeful. The paper given by Jacob Viner at the Chicago conference, cited earlier, was one such example. Even Viner, however, had suggested that the "wretched" gold standard might be necessary.

The economic contraction did not end in 1932. The Federal Reserve Board half-heartedly initiated some open market purchases of government securities in mid-1932, largely in response to the Chicago conference, and continued them for a few months. Just as some small signs of recovery appeared, however, the Board abandoned the open market purchase policy and went back to real-bills-as-usual (see Friedman and Schwartz 1963: 420–91). The downward spiral of the economy continued through the elections of late 1932 and contributed to significant losses for incumbent Republican politicians, including President Herbert Hoover.

The new president, Franklin D. Roosevelt, and the Democratic Congress that came into power with him were determined to right the ship of state. Their New Deal program called for direct and positive spending by existing and newly created government agencies. In addition, to counteract the contractionary gold standard monetary system that all parties—however erroneously—agreed was at fault, congressional committees and the executive initiated "resolutions" and changes in laws to eliminate gold from the monetary picture. Gold, however, was well understood to be a constitutional fixture and could not so easily be abandoned.

Even before the New Deal sought to dismantle gold, the Hoover administration and the Republican Congress of early 1932 had tried to circumvent Federal Reserve policy. They introduced and passed the Reconstruction Finance Corporation Act. This new agency was capitalized with $500 million of general taxpayer revenues and could issue its own bonds and debentures to raise three times as much. Its mission was to lend to banks, corporations, and government agencies that "could not get help from conventional sources" (White 1935: 697–702).

The most obvious "conventional sources" were the 12 Federal Reserve banks. They had been the touted lenders of last resort, but during the Great Contraction of 1929–1933 had turned out to be lenders of no resort. Since the Fed banks were still regarded as elements of the private banking system, their lending actions were treated as if they were somehow those of private, even profit-making, institutions. Indeed, the Fed banks occasionally realized some net returns, faced reserve requirements, and seemed to operate within the commercial banking system—as Miller, Willis, and other real bills proponents had argued they should.

The Reconstruction Finance Corporation was supposed to provide an answer to the nonlending of the Fed banks. It "should extend loans to banks on assets not now eligible for rediscount at the Federal reserve banks" (U.S. Department of the Treasury 1931: 34). As Secretary of the Treasury Ogden Mills explained in his 1932 report, "What the Government did in creating the Reconstruction Finance Corporation was to put the credit of the Government itself back of the national credit structure" (U.S. Department of the Treasury 1932: 327–29). Just a year earlier, Treasury Secretary Andrew Mellon had stated that commercial banks had $3.2 billion of eligible paper and $4.5 billion of U.S. government securities, all of which was eligible to serve "as a basis for additional Federal Reserve Bank accommodation" (White 1935: 48).

Clearly, the commercial banks' eligible paper had not been exhausted. Reserve bank loan committees had, first, punished "speculation," and then, reflecting the depressed state of business that followed, in which no loans looked "eligible," continued their stinginess. The absence of new production meant to them that no money was needed. All the published works of the real bills advocates reflected this argument.

The Reconstruction Finance Corporation was simply a quasi-bank lending institution in lieu of Fed banks that "were unable to help." It could "help" because it was allowed to broaden the eligibility concept to include assets that were "sound" and "acceptable" even if not real bills. However, its net effect on the monetary system was nil because, unlike the Fed banks, it had no independent means to create bank reserves and currency. At best, it could only promise relief through its claim on taxpayers' resources. But even that promise was almost nonexistent by this time.

One month after Congress passed the Reconstruction Finance Act it also passed the Glass-Steagall Act (February 27, 1932). The act permitted Fed banks to use government securities as collateral for Federal Reserve notes, thereby compromising the original real bills feature of the Federal Reserve Act. By this amendment the act "freed up" almost $1 billion of gold serving as a dollar-for-dollar backing of Federal Reserve notes and reserves for member bank deposits. The new act also enabled the Fed banks to assist the Treasury in managing recurring fiscal deficits, some of which were due to Treasury financing of the Reconstruction Finance Corporation. By this means, a significant amount of Fed-held gold was liberated for other purposes (White 1935: 702–5). However, even with the former shackles on Fed bank gold certificate reserves, the Fed banks had all the gold they could have needed for reversing the contraction. It was not a lack of gold, but the Fed's real bills *counter-speculation* thinking that was the problem.

In early 1933, before the new administration took office, the economy suffered its third banking crisis since 1929 (Friedman and Schwartz 1963: 324–49). The new Congress quickly passed an Emergency Banking Act, and President Roosevelt signed it into law on March 9, 1933, a few days after he took office. The act allowed the president to declare a "banking holiday," which he did immediately, shutting down the entire banking system and causing more financial havoc. Even routine bank clearing operations came to a halt. The act also gave the executive, through the Treasury Department, the power to call in all gold coins and gold certificates owned domestically, to be reimbursed at the prevailing gold price of $20.67 per ounce—the price that had been in effect since 1834 (White 1935: 705).

On April 5, 1933, President Roosevelt issued Executive Order 6102, which fulfilled this provision of the Banking Act. The order required all American citizens to turn in all gold coins, gold bullion, and gold certificates to the U.S. Treasury, to be redeemed in nongold dollars—that is, greenbacks, silver certificates, or any other government-issued currency—at the gold dollar price of $20.67 per ounce.

Finally, on April 20, 1933, the federal government officially abandoned the gold standard in the United States. Any debt owed by the United States could be paid in any paper currency that the federal government in the past had been authorized to issue. No one could now demand gold in payment for any government debt. All government paper money was "legal tender for all debts public and private." Period. By this time gold exports and gold "hoarding" were also largely prohibited (White 1935: 733).[1]

The legislative barrage continued. In May 1933, Congress passed the Thomas Amendment to an Agricultural Adjustment Act that authorized (and encouraged) Fed banks to buy $3 billion of government securities— a simple open market purchase. With the securities as collateral, the Fed banks were to issue $3 billion in Federal Reserve notes. Unfortunately, the Fed Board thwarted this potential relief. Open market operations to increase the money supply were still anathema to the real bills stalwarts on the Fed Board, and they still dominated Fed policies. The Thomas Amendment also gave the president authority to reduce the gold content of the dollar—that is, to deflate the gold dollar—thereby raising the mint price of gold, as expressed in dollars, by as much as 60 percent (White 1935: 709–10). This power was not used until about a year later.

Congress took the next step on June 5, 1933, passing a joint resolution that "expressly voided the gold clauses in all public and private bonds, mortgages, and contracts" (White 1935: 712–13). Gold

---

[1] The law made exception for a limited amount of numismatic gold coin possession, as well as for $100 worth of gold per individual for any purpose.

clauses were statements inserted in both private and government debt contracts that promised repayment of the debt in either standard gold money or the gold equivalent in other dollars—silver coins or certificates, national banknotes, and U.S. notes (greenbacks)—at the option of the bondholder (White 1935: 712–13).

A few weeks later, in mid-June, Congress passed the Banking Act of 1933 (White 1935: 714). One of the main provisions of this act gave additional powers to the Fed Board and Fed banks to oversee loans and investments of member banks, to prevent "speculative" trading in securities, commodities, and real estate from crowding out "legitimate" credit for other borrowers. The act pointedly exempted all security issues of the federal government, state governments, and government agencies from the "speculative" class of securities (White 1935: 715).[2] Even after five years of anti-speculative disaster, the real bills bugaboo of "speculation" was still undermining rational monetary policy.

The path was now clear for the federal government to take possession of all the country's monetary gold. On January 30, 1934, Congress passed the Gold Reserve Act. On January 31, President Roosevelt, using the authority vested in him by the act passed the previous day and the resolution passed seven months earlier, reduced the gold content of the dollar by more than 59 percent, thereby raising the official (or mint) price of gold from $20.67 to $35 per ounce.

While the devaluation sounded good for gold owners, the Gold Reserve Act also authorized the Treasury to call in all monetary gold, including that held by reserve banks, to be reimbursed at the old price of $20.67 per ounce. As a result of these edicts, the U.S. Treasury realized a "profit" of $2.8 billion on its new gold holdings, an amount almost as great as annual federal tax revenues at that time. Much of the Treasury gold was committed to an Exchange Stabilization Fund under the control of the secretary of the Treasury. Thus none of the

---

[2] This act also created the Federal Deposit Insurance Corporation. By October 1, 1934, 98 percent of all deposit accounts in U.S. banks were fully insured. The act included several other important measures as well: the complete separation of investment and commercial banking, regulation of bank holding companies, increases in minimum capital requirements for national banks, and other restrictions on member banks' freedom to manage their enterprises.

gold "profit" was available for current fiscal operations or for any private purpose (White 1935: 720–21).

Devaluation of the gold dollar so that the value of the stock of gold, now in the hands of the government, would be greatly enhanced was another episode in the "war on gold." It was the government saying to the gold standard: "You won't produce the quantity of money that you are supposed to produce. Therefore, we will produce it for you by legislating new money in your name."

If *the* gold standard could have replied, she would have said, "I wanted to produce much more money without such an unconstitutional law, but that villain"—pointing to Dr. Real Bills—"wouldn't let me. Every time I tried to create more money, he would block me. He kept complaining that the paper I wanted to use as collateral for my new money was either designed to aid speculators, or that it didn't have the look of a loan that was short term and promoting the production of real goods."

Our villain might have replied: "I was not being obstructive. The Federal Reserve Act, which initiated my role as a lender of last resort, specified that I was to create 'credit' only when production facilities needed assistance for that type of loan. If productive enterprise is apathetic, and no one wants to produce anything, I can't help it. That just shows that no new money is needed."

A properly functioning gold standard would have dominated any presumptive real bills effort to control speculation so that no ensuing depression could have occurred. Speculators who were wrong would have become ex-speculators and looked for other jobs, while those who had speculated profitably would have been rewarded and become financiers.

The Treasury, adhering to the terms of the act and the resolution, had all the gold it collected melted down and recast into ingots, each of which weighed approximately 27.5 pounds. Collecting, melting, and casting the gold into ingots cost a significant number of depression dollars and rendered the gold unfit for any monetary function. The whole process was analogous to a government mandate calling for everyone to turn in washing machines, or any useful household device, which would be paid for at the prevailing value of used machinery, and which the government would then turn into bales of scrap metal. The metal would still be there, but the utility of the machinery would be destroyed. Since gold could no longer be used to redeem or serve as a reserve for any common money—in fact, the new law made it illegal for such purposes—gold could not "back" money. The new ingots had utility only as ballast to hold down the floor at Ft. Knox and other gold depositories.

The scene after 1934 shifted to the role played by the Treasury Department in the management of gold. The Treasury held some gold reserves against its own currency obligations—U.S. notes (greenbacks), its issues of gold and silver certificates, and in small part national banknotes. It also held gold, dollar-for-dollar, for the gold certificate assets of Fed banks, which were in turn a reserve for Federal Reserve notes outstanding and for the reserve accounts of member banks, which in turn gave rise to commercial banks' demand deposits. In short, the actual gold, now concentrated in Treasury vaults, was the accounting base on which all bank reserves, bank deposits, and hand-to-hand currency rested. However, no common money could be redeemed for gold, and no private person or institution could use the gold as money.

As Table 3 showed, the Treasury's gold holdings were substantial and increased steadily through the 1920s and the early 1930s. Then the arithmetic of gold dollar devaluation caused exceptional dollar increases in Treasury gold holdings. By 1942 the Treasury's gold stock was worth more than $22 billion and weighed well over 19,000 tons.[3]

The mechanics of changes in gold stocks on the quantity of common money were as follows:

Gold inflows had to come into the monetary system through the Treasury to be "monetized." When the Treasury Department bought

[3] If this gold had been loaded into 10-ton trucks, it would have required 1,900 trucks. Then, if the trucks formed a convoy with 100 feet between the front bumpers of each truck, the convoy would have stretched out for *36 miles*. About half of this gold, however, was on deposit and the property of foreign governments and nationals, who had sent the gold to the United States for safekeeping.

the gold, it issued gold certificates specifying the dollar value of the newly imported gold. It also wrote a check of equal dollar value payable to the former owner of the gold.

The Treasury then deposited the new gold certificates in Federal Reserve banks. The Fed banks, in keeping with the original Federal Reserve Act, held these certificates as their "primary reserves." Gold certificates were a paper "currency" like many others, except that they were in hundred-thousand-dollar denominations.

The sellers of the gold now had checks receivable that they deposited in commercial banks, which duly sent the checks on to their district Fed banks for credit to their reserve accounts. Thus, the checks that the Treasury paid for the gold created reserves for member banks on the basis of which they were able to make additional loans and investments. If the seller of the gold wanted ordinary currency— that is, Federal Reserve notes—then the Fed bank that had the new gold certificates could issue Federal Reserve notes dollar-for-dollar to redeem the checks.

The net changes in the monetary aggregates due to a gold inflow, after all the debits and credits had canceled out, were (1) a given dollar increase in the gold certificate accounts of Fed banks, and (2) an equal dollar increase in the reserve accounts of member banks, or (3) a similar increase in Federal Reserve notes outstanding if the recipient of the checks wanted currency. The Treasury's hoard of gold metal increased as well.

THE GOLD CLAUSE CASES

The war on gold had one final chapter, the gold clause cases, which resulted from the 59 percent devaluation of the gold dollar in January 1934. Both government and private debts often included "gold clauses" that gave the creditor of the debt the right to demand either current dollars or gold when the debt matured and was redeemed. Since the devaluation of the gold dollar had raised the price of gold significantly, both private and public creditors were looking at a dollar windfall gain when their debtors had to pay. The inevitable happened and creditors demanded gold (or its equivalent in dollars) for payment. Both private debtors and the U.S. Treasury refused, and the cases trying them soon came to the Supreme Court.

The major and underlying problem, which was not addressed or treated in the court cases, was the magnitude of the gold devaluation that Congress had just passed. Congress's power to change the gold or silver content of the dollar—implied by the words ". . . coin money and *regulate* the value thereof" in the Constitution—meant only that Congress could *adjust* the gold content of gold coins or the silver content of silver coins by a very small percentage, so that both coins would stay current in circulation.[4] Devaluation was to be used only rarely to keep an array of currency denominations in circulation. It was not intended to be used as a sorcerer's wand to flood the monetary system with new money.

The gold clause cases, which tested the constitutionality of the retraction of gold clauses from contracts, went to the Supreme Court in January 1935. The Court decided by a 5–4 majority that the devaluation law was constitutional. The majority opinion, delivered by Chief Justice Charles Evans Hughes, upheld the constitutionality of the government's denial of gold for payment, even when a gold clause was clearly written into the contract. As Chief Justice Hughes put it, "We [the majority] are not concerned with their wisdom [of the gold clauses as a policy]. The question before the Court is one of power [of Congress], not of policy." Did Congress have the power to deny windfall gold payments for redemption of the debt contracts (Timberlake 2013: 189–90)?

Hughes first cited Congress's explicit constitutional authority "to coin money and regulate the value thereof." Then he introduced the opinions from the legal tender cases argued in 1870–1871 and 1884. Those three cases decided whether the greenbacks issued in 1862 and 1863 were legitimate tender for clearing debts made before passage of

---

[4] For a complete discussion of constitutional devaluation, see Timberlake (2013: 35–39). A very important problem with the currency during most of the 19th century was the paucity—even the disappearance—of small denomination coins.

the Legal Tender Acts. The first decision, rendered in 1870, decided by a 5–3 majority that they were not—that a debt incurred before the acts were passed had to be paid off with gold if the creditor chose.

At that time the Court had two vacancies. President Ulysses Grant, thereupon, appointed two new justices to the Court whose judgments on similar cases at the state level had favored the constitutionality of the greenbacks under *any* conditions. The revamped Court then retried the case and—no surprise—reversed the earlier decision by a 5–4 vote. It found the greenbacks constitutional under any circumstances as legal tender for clearing debts no matter when a debt was incurred. A third decision in 1884, with a Court similarly biased, confirmed the previous decision by an 8–1 majority (Timberlake 2013: 86–113).[5]

The critical argument in both the 1871 and 1884 decisions granting Congress omnipotent power to print money claimed that the Constitution was written to establish and maintain a sovereign government ruled by Congress. Congress's monetary authority had to be sufficient "... to achieve the great objects on which the government was framed—a national government with sovereign powers ... [that could] issue the obligations of the United States in such form ... as accord with the usage of sovereign governments" (Timberlake 2013: 191).[6]

Absolutely nothing in the Constitution nor in the Bill of Rights states or even implies any such power leading to this interpretation. "Sovereign government" is nowhere to be found in either document. Only a limited and critically defined sovereignty was allowed the federal government; all other issues of sovereignty were reserved for the states or the people.

The 1935 Court minority then had its turn to pass judgment on the gold clause cases. Four dissenting justices denounced the majority opinion. Their objections, written and read by Justice James McReynolds, began with the statement that the majority opinion

[5] All the justices who had supported limited greenback constitutionality had left the Court and had been replaced by pro-greenbackers. Only Justice Stephen Field remained from the former group

[6] To appreciate completely the fatuous nonsense of the 1871 and 1884 Court decisions validating Congress's issues of greenbacks as constitutional, one must read the full decisions.

"would bring about the confiscation of property rights and repudiation of national obligations." The minority saw the denial of gold redemption for debts with gold clauses as the act of a deceitful government that had taken the authority "to annihilate its own obligations and destroy the very rights which the Founders were endeavoring to protect. Not only is there no permission for such actions," the minority countered, but "they are inhibited. And no plentitude of words can conform them to our [constitutional] charter."

McReynolds reviewed the pedigree of the gold clause in both the United States and foreign countries. It was there, he lectured, ". . . to protect against a depreciation of the currency and against the discharge of obligations by payment of less than that prescribed." He noted that the "calculation to determine the damages for failure to pay [at the new price of gold] would not be difficult"—that is, multiply the face value of the debt by 1.69, the ratio of the gold value of the new gold dollars to the old gold dollars. (Timberlake 2013: 199).

Both the majority and minority opinions reflected the impossible constitutionality of the case. The Hughes majority would have done economic justice to the debtor-creditor relationship by having the debtor pay justly in real terms, but it would thereby have violated the gold option in the contract. The McReynolds minority would have allowed the appreciation of all gold-based contractual debts by the devaluation ratio. Bondholder creditors would have profited by 69 percent, plus some amount due to the decline in prices that had occurred over most of this era. Clearly, this decision would have resulted in the "undeserved enrichment" of all bondholders, but that was what any gold dollar devaluation would do under a gold standard.[7] That also is why devaluations were not everyday occurrences under a true gold standard, and why they were very small when they did occur.[8]

[7] As Table 1 shows, prices rose about 60 percent from 1917 to 1920 but then stayed virtually constant until 1930. They then began a steady decline until 1933, at which time they were back to their 1917 level. So any bond that was purchased in the 1920s would have appreciated significantly in real terms by 1934 and by an additional 69 percent due to the gold dollar devaluation.

[8] The gold devaluation of 1834, the only other devaluation in U.S. monetary experience, increased the price of gold by 6.6 percent, an amount that was witheringly criticized by a later monetary historian (see McCulloch 1994: 57–67).

More important, however, is the point that the majority found its rationale for the gold dollar devaluation, and the abrogation of the gold clause, in Congress's "sovereign" power over the monetary system, which the Court decisions in 1871 and 1884 had fallaciously given it. This misinterpretation of the Constitution and the misjudgment in the legal tender decisions became the basis for sanctioning the decision in 1935 (see Timberlake 2013: 129–55). Unwittingly, the McReynolds-led dissenters agreed on this crucial point. "There is no challenge here of the power of Congress to adopt such proper 'Monetary Policy' as it may deem necessary in order to provide for national obligations and furnish an adequate medium of exchange for public use," McReynolds read. That is, both majority and minority opinions— all nine justices—agreed that the majority's arguments in the legal tender cases of 1870–1871 and 1884 were constitutional. McReynolds continued, "The conclusions there announced are not now questioned; and any abstract discussion of Congressional power over money would only tend to befog the issue" (Timberlake 2013: 200).

But would it "befog the issue"? Here was a perfect place for judicial review of the legal tender decisions of 1871 and 1884. The Supreme Court is the highest tribunal for interpreting constitutional law, which means that its decisions can have no review by lower courts. However, Supreme Court justices are human and can make both errors of judgment and errors because of their political biases. Given these obvious possibilities, what means or procedures are available to lessen or correct such mistakes?

The simplest and probably only means is judicial review, especially if a questionable and controversial previous decision has an important bearing on a contemporary case. Given an unpalatable decision that a later Court believes is both faulty and important in deciding a new case, the Court can and should reconsider and reargue the original decision. That is, in fact, precisely what the Supreme Court did in the legal tender cases of 1870–1871 and 1884. When it considered *Knox v. Lee* and *Parker v. Davis* in 1870–1871, it reversed the 1869 decision it had made in *Hepburn v. Griswold.* The Court then reaffirmed its reversed decision in 1884 in *Juilliard v. Greenman* (Timberlake 2013: 86–114, 221–27).

Justice William Strong, the author of the majority decision in 1871, realizing that the Court was reviewing as well as reversing the *Hepburn* decision, had the grace to be indulgent as well as rational. "These [legal tender] cases," he advised in his majority discussion, "are constitutional questions of vital importance to the government and to the public. . . . [If] convinced we made a mistake, we would hear another argument and correct our error. And it is no unprecedented thing in courts of last resort, both in this country and in England, to overrule decisions previously made" (Timberlake 2013: 227).

Just as the Strong-led majority in 1871 had overruled *Hepburn*, so the Hughes Court in 1935 could have properly reexamined the legal tender cases. On that basis the full Court could have argued that the devaluation itself was unconstitutional and that the legislative branch had to come up with something reasonable. While such a course might not have been politically appealing, it would have enabled the Court to avoid a decision on a case that offered no constitutional monetary solution.

Thus the answer here is that *there was no answer*. The case could not be litigated because the magnitude of the unprecedented devaluation was implicitly unconstitutional and that issue was not treated—or even mentioned.

The Supreme Court's mistaken acceptance of Congress's absolute power over the monetary system in 1935, without heed to gold standard constraints, gave Congress the incentive and the license to get in the game and "do something" about the Great Depression that had already lasted six years. Using its newly discovered powers, Congress initiated and passed the Banking Act of 1935 on August 23 of that year. The institutional changes and monetary policies resulting from that act conclude the saga of the Real Bills Doctrine and spell the end of the end for the gold standard.

13

THE (CENTRAL) BANKING ACT OF 1935

By early 1935, the monetary thinking and policies that the Real Bills Doctrine had inspired were beginning to fade away. J. Laurence Laughlin, the original publicist for the Real Bills Doctrine, died in 1933. Adolph Miller, a student of Laughlin's and the most prominent official promoting real bills policy in the early 1930s, had retired from the Fed Board. H. Parker Willis, a devoted real bills advocate who was the first secretary of the Federal Reserve Board (1914–1918), was teaching at Columbia University but would die in 1937. Willis's intellectual influence in favor of the Real Bills Doctrine was still evident in 1935 but had lost its previous relevance.

However, the most politically influential "real billser," Sen. Carter Glass of Virginia, was still in office. Glass was a close associate of Willis and, with Miller, had helped him write a major part of the Federal Reserve Act. He was chair of the House Banking and Currency Committee when that act was written and became chair of the Senate Finance Committee after he moved to the Senate. He dominated banking legislation the whole time he was in Congress. Indeed, it would have been fair to describe him as "Senator Real Bills"—all his arguments and policies were colored by real bills principles.

Nonetheless, adherence to the Real Bills Doctrine was in retreat. Throughout the Great Contraction and into 1935, real bills proponents had perpetuated the notion that the production of real goods and services arises first in the real economy by a sort of parthenogenetic mixture of inspiration, creativity, and hard work—what Keynes in his *General Theory* called "animal spirits"—which then is funded by the creation of bank credit. This theory, though a harmless banking principle for an economy ruled by a gold standard, had no applicability to

an economy that had lost its gold standard directive and its entrepreneurial capabilities and was in an advanced state of production paraly-
sis. Such a depressed and demonetized economy could not generate
any real bills. Its problem was primarily a dearth of money.

More immediately, the Supreme Court ruling on the gold clause
cases had effectively granted Congress complete sovereign power over
the monetary system. The role required Congress to provide a revised
institutional directive for Federal Reserve policy, since the Fed was
obviously the agency that would manage the government's newly
discovered monetary powers. Accordingly, a new banking act would
shift the ends and means of monetary policy to a Fed that would be
endowed with the appropriate authority to fulfill them.

The government's gold-control mindset continued under the
Roosevelt administration. When he took office in 1933, Roosevelt
had appointed Henry Morgenthau, a long-time acquaintance and
friend, to be governor of the Federal Farm Board. Morgenthau was
a conservative who believed in the gold standard—as did most of the
administration.

Morgenthau became one of Roosevelt's closest advisers. In 1934,
he and a few other of Roosevelt's "insiders" manipulated the daily
increase in the price of gold that led to the gold dollar devaluation in
January 1934 and the subsequent Supreme Court decision confirm-
ing its constitutionality. Morgenthau later remarked that, "If anybody
ever knew how we set the price of gold through a combination of
lucky numbers, etc., I think that they would be really frightened" (see
Richardson, Komai, and Gou 2013).[1]

In 1934, Roosevelt upgraded Morgenthau to Secretary of the
Treasury. Besides being an advocate for the gold standard, Morgenthau
allegedly favored balanced budgets and fiscal responsibility. To fur-
ther these objectives, he suggested to Roosevelt the appointment of
Marriner Eccles, a close adviser, as the new chairman of the Fed
Board, and Roosevelt duly appointed him.

---

[1] The method Morgenthau referred to was the random drawing of playing cards by the president to
determine the daily percentage increase in the price of gold.

Eccles was a commercial banker from Utah. He argued forcefully that the Fed should "support expansionary fiscal policy through discretionary monetary policy" (quoted in Kettl 1986: 48). For him, the front door of the Treasury would also be the back door to the Fed.[2] Eccles's fiscal-first, activist approach to monetary policy was what recommended him for the Fed chairmanship, even though he held some views contrary to Morgenthau's.

After Eccles became chair, he brought in as his assistant director of research Lauchlin Currie, who had a recent PhD in economics from Harvard. Currie was well-known for his research on the quantity theory of money (see also Sandilands 1990). Fresh from his doctoral studies, Currie had anticipated some of the later arguments of Friedman and Schwartz as well as the authors of the present volume (see Laidler 1999). In a series of writings from 1929 to 1934, Currie emphasized six important points: (1) He called attention to the flaws of the Real Bills Doctrine, which he called "the commercial loan theory of banking." (2) He distinguished between this doctrine and the quantity theory of money, which he cited favorably in the late 1920s and early 1930s. (3) He emphasized that the Fed Board had stubbornly adhered to the Real Bills Doctrine, most especially to its anti-speculation requirement. (4) He stressed that using a policy of anti-speculation as a barrier to Fed assistance was largely responsible for the Fed Board's inaction in preventing the wave of bank failures, and for letting the money supply shrink during 1929–1933. (5) Such monetary contraction, he pointed out, caused the Great Depression. (6) And he distinguished between "money" and "credit," noting that money refers to the liquid items on the liability side of bank balance sheets and credit to the loan and investment accounts on the asset side (see Laidler 1999).

That Currie is not properly recognized today as a key precursor of the monetarist explanation of the depression is largely due to his own apostasy: He abandoned the quantity theory as a policy guide when he went to Washington to work, first, for Marriner Eccles at

---

[2] Since the Federal Reserve Board was housed in the Treasury building until 1936, this construct was more real than imagined.

the Fed Board and, later, for President Roosevelt in the White House. In the mid-1930s and beyond, he abandoned his belief in what monetary policy could accomplish and became a Keynesian advocate of fiscal deficits and redistributionist budget policy. Nonetheless, Currie merits a place in the short list of monetarist scholars who had some significant understanding of the causal role of the Real Bills Doctrine in the Great Depression.

Together, Eccles and Currie argued that the forthcoming banking act should equip the Fed to promote "conscious [monetary] control." The Federal Reserve Board of Governors in Washington—rather than the 12 regional Fed bank presidents—ought to be the primary decisionmaking body, according to this view (Kettl 1986, 48–53). Every business experience was different, Eccles and Currie argued, and required conscious human adaptation. Therefore, the "handling of the instruments of control must be discretionary" (Kettl 1986: 50).[3] This statement neglects completely any reference to a gold standard or to a market-determined money. It is an argument that has been a staple of central banking apologists for 100 years.

The Banking Act of 1935 was introduced in the House of Representatives in February 1935 and passed in August that year. During its controversial journey through Congress, the bill was subjected to many amendments and much debate over its details.[4] Fed chair Eccles was especially zealous in his attempts to secure an act that reflected his and Currie's idea of centering control of policy in a strong Fed Board—rather than leaving the Fed banks as policymaking institutions able to treat problems in their own districts at their own discretion. Many members of Congress also supported centralized control by the Fed Board, coupled with a monetary policy that would adapt to the spending demands of the Treasury Department (see Timberlake 1993: 282–87).[5]

[3] Memo from Currie to Eccles, April 1935.

[4] For a complete treatment of this act, see Friedman and Schwartz (1963: 445–62).

[5] At the time many observers believed that the Federal Reserve System was a part of the commercial banking system and not a special credit-controlling agency. Therefore, a "banking act" could apply to both commercial banks and the Fed banks. After the Banking Act of 1935 passed, however, the Fed banks became a central banking system—no qualification needed.

Rep. Henry Steagall, a Democratic representative from Alabama, was chair of the House Committee on Banking and Currency that would frame the new act. He and Senator Glass, chair of the Senate Finance Committee, therefore had to synthesize their views into an acceptable bill.

At first, Glass was highly critical of the legislation because it minimized the real bills criterion, which had been the original basis for Fed policy. Steagall, however, favored the bill for the same reason. He remarked, correctly, that many member banks during the recent banking crises "went down in ruins because of the arbitrary, inelastic, straitlaced eligibility requirements of the Federal Reserve System, as a result of which solvent banks were unable to get the accommodations to which they were entitled."[6] By 1935, this view was shared by most members of Congress, as well as by many economists in academia and business.

The solution Steagall offered was not to abolish the Fed and go back to a gold standard without any central bank, but instead to replace the wrong people—the Federal Reserve "bankers" who Steagall thought had been directing Fed policy—with the right people. The proposed law allowed the president to reconstitute the Fed Board and reconfigure the Federal Open Market Committee (FOMC). According to Steagall, this change would bring "the System with its vast resources into full harmony with the advanced policies of the present Administration." "We all know," Steagall concluded in a classic statement of men versus law, "that it does not matter so much what we write into the law as it does who administers the law." By diverting control of the system from the 12 Fed banks to the nine-man Fed Board in Washington, monetary policy could, Steagall supposed, be carried out in the name of the "people of the United States."[7]

In response, Senator Glass began by referring to Steagall as the "worst inflationist in the country." Glass had become a conservative brake against monetary activism. He argued that the FOMC, which

---

[6] *Congressional Record*, 74th Cong., 1st sess., p. 13706. Steagall did not connect this proper criticism, however, to the real bills policies of Miller and the Fed Board.

[7] *Congressional Record*, 74th Cong., 1st sess., p. 13706.

was getting additional powers in the Banking Act of 1935, was only supposed to enhance Fed banks' discount rates—the primary method of monetary control. "It is now presumed," he rasped, "to make the open-market committee the supreme power in the determination of the credits [i.e., money supply] of the country. No such thing was intended [by the Federal Reserve Act] and no such thing should ever be done." The Board of Governors, which would staff the new open market committee, he said, "does not have a dollar of pecuniary interest in the Reserve funds or the deposits of the Federal Reserve Banks or of the member banks."[8]

In this statement, Glass was reflecting his own real bills–colored view of the original Fed. The eligible paper doctrine had proven over the preceding six years to be not only unworkable but positively stultifying to the economy. When the economy was booming, all discounted paper was very, very "eligible." But then sometimes, as in late 1929 and after, such paper was tainted by speculation that made it horrid.

The new banking bill would not require Fed banks to discount paper or make other policy decisions, and the "eligible paper" criterion would no longer be limiting. The Real Bills Doctrine had itself proven toxic—not to Senator Glass and a few other hard-liners, such as H. Parker Willis, but to populist legislators whose purpose now was to restore the economy's money supply, which had somehow disappeared. The new banking act would feature open market operations in government securities under the control of the FOMC, which would be largely appointed by the president.[9]

This issue sparked a controversy in the Senate over who and what bodies in the Federal Reserve System should and did have control of policy. The two debaters were Senator Glass and Sen. Elmer Thomas, a Democrat and populist from Oklahoma. Thomas had become

---

[8] *Congressional Record*, 74th Cong., 1st sess., p. 11778.

[9] The president would appoint five members to the new committee, while four members would be presidents (no longer "governors") of the Fed banks. Membership would rotate, with the president of the Fed Bank of New York a permanent member.

noteworthy for his 1933 amendment, which had provided for the issue of $3 billion of unsupported greenbacks.[10]

"The Federal Reserve Board," said Thomas, "should be the most powerful, the most important, and most respected tribunal in the United States." Unfortunately, he continued, the Board as then authorized did not control the policies of the Federal Reserve System. Rather, "the policy of the 12 banks is controlled and dictated by the Federal Reserve Bank of New York."[11] While he meant well, Thomas was reflecting the confused set of precepts governing the system: Until 1929, the Fed Bank of New York had largely controlled Fed policy. However, after that date, the real bills–inspired Fed Board was in control. Without understanding the difference that this shift in power implied, Thomas's observation reflected his and the general public's misunderstanding of the ongoing disaster.

Glass denied Thomas's statement as "inaccurate . . . [and] a humiliating confession that the Federal Reserve Board . . . declined to assert its lawful functions. . . . The Board was instituted to see that the Federal Reserve Banks obeyed the law."

Thomas replied, "Heretofore, the Federal Reserve Board has been so circumscribed with limitations that [it] had virtually no effective power."

Glass: "They had all power."[12]

The two senators' conflicting concepts of what monetary policies were and had been, and who controlled policy, illustrate that these details had never been properly specified, either in the Federal Reserve Act or after. Indeed, the presence of a conventional, working gold standard did not *require* any designed monetary policy. No policy was needed because the gold standard itself *was* the monetary policy. Only an operational central bank would require specifications about

<hr>

[10] The Thomas amendment was a provision in the Banking Act of May 12, 1933, giving the president the authority to issue $3 billion in U.S. notes—greenbacks—with no collateral behind them, as well as the authority to devalue the gold dollar. The gold dollar was devalued, but the greenbacks were never issued.

[11] *Congressional Record*, 74th Cong., 1st sess., pp. 11923–24 (1935). Of course, the Fed Board was not a "tribunal." It had nine members.

[12] *Congressional Record*, 74th Cong., 1st sess., pp. 11923–24.

monetary policy, and in this respect the Federal Reserve Act of 1913 had proven critically inadequate.

Senator Thomas, by his next words, correctly implied that no gold standard was or had been operational for some time. He complained at length that, "Someone, somewhere has been and is regulating the value [of money]; and I should like to inquire under what law is the value of the dollar being regulated?" This dollar, he observed, had doubled in value—that is, the price level had fallen by 50 percent—from "unknown causes" between 1920 and 1935. "There is no authority, there is no commission, there is no board, there is no particular individual who has had enjoined on it or him, by congressional mandate, the duty of regulating the value of the dollar." His prescription was that the Fed Board be "charged with this responsibility."[13]

By comparing the real value of the dollar for the two years 1920 and 1935 as though some consistent policy was in place, Thomas again showed that he did not realize how different factions in the Federal Reserve System had taken charge of policy during the period in question—how Benjamin Strong's quantity theory of money–inspired New York Fed had given way to Adolph Miller's Real Bills Doctrine Fed Board. Thomas was not alone in his ignorance; in fact, his misunderstanding seemed almost universal.

Following Thomas's remarks, two other senators, Gerald Nye of North Dakota and William Borah of Montana, proposed amending the bill to require the new Fed Board to maintain a stable price level. Nye even wanted the Board's staff to include the Bureau of Labor Statistics, so that the Board could "scientifically and accurately determine the rate at which additions to the stock of circulating money . . . must be made in order to maintain an even and stable purchasing power!"[14] The Senate rejected Nye's and Borah's proposed amendments by a voice vote. Senators foresaw an enlarged role for the new Fed, but a price level rule to make policy objective was not sufficient for the

[13] *Congressional Record*, 74th Cong., 1st sess., p. 11925. Thomas did not realize that Governor Strong and the Fed Bank of New York had followed just this policy through the 1920s—possibly because Strong did not advertise it as such.

[14] *Congressional Record*, 74th Cong., 1st sess., p. 11842.

discretionary spending programs that they and the Roosevelt administration anticipated.

The Banking Act of 1935 fundamentally changed the original Federal Reserve Act.[15] Changes in the means and methods of monetary policy included the following:

First, the FOMC was reorganized to include the seven members of the Fed Board and 5 of the 12 Fed bank presidents, who would rotate on and off the FOMC, with the president of the New York Fed a permanent member. From this time on, only the Fed Board and the FOMC had policymaking powers. The FOMC would carry out all open market operations using the New York Fed as its operating agent.

Second, the Fed Board was authorized to set reserve requirements for member banks. Up to this time, reserve requirements for member banks had been statutorily fixed at 7 percent for "country" banks, 10 percent for reserve city banks—"reserve cities" included all major cities except New York and Chicago—and 13 percent for member banks in the central reserve cities of New York and Chicago. Reserve requirements were determined not by a bank's size, but by its location. The new act gave the Fed Board power to alter these requirements within a range between the previously fixed percentages and double those percentages: that is, 7–14 percent for country banks, 10–20 percent for reserve city banks, and 13–26 percent for member banks in New York and Chicago.

By this act, the Federal Reserve System ceased to be a special section of the commercial banking system. It became instead a full-fledged central bank with complete control over the economy's stock of money. It has remained so ever since.

---

[15] For a rigorous evaluation of these changes, see Friedman and Schwartz (1963: 445–49).

$$\text{(14)}$$

BANK RESERVE REQUIREMENTS
AND THE RECESSION OF 1937–1938

The terrible turmoil anticipating war in Europe in the mid-1930s prompted many European states, institutions, and individuals to send their gold to the United States for safekeeping. Consequently, large imports of gold kept showing up on the U.S. Treasury's balance sheet—by this time the only legal avenue gold could take as it came into the United States.

The gold imports kept coming both before and after passage of the Banking Act of 1935. In 1932, the Fed banks' gold certificate account was $3.15 billion. By 1936, that account stood at $8.02 billion, reflecting these inflows as well as the devaluation noted above, and was continuing to increase (see Table 3). On net balance, the gold inflow increased the stock of common money (i.e., hand-to-hand currency and deposits subject to check in commercial and saving banks) from 1933 through 1936, at annual rates of 9.5 percent, 14.0 percent, and 13.0 percent, respectively (Friedman and Schwartz 1963: 544).

The commercial member banks, however, were not doing their part. While expanding business loans and investments, they were also building up excess reserves—that is, reserves that exceeded the minimum legal reserve requirement percentages fixed by the Fed Board of Governors in accordance with the new Banking Act of 1935. By December 1935, member banks were accounting in their balance sheets more excess reserves than required reserves: Total reserves were more than double the legally required amount.

This condition reflected the experience of bankers who had survived the catastrophic experiences of the Great Contraction just a few years earlier. Then, owing to the Federal Reserve's failure to provide sufficient last-resort liquidity to help banks cover panic-driven runs on their deposits, over 9,000 commercial banks had been bankrupted. The bankers who were left were doubly conservative. First, as Friedman and Schwartz observed, their survival through 1930–1933 was due in large part to their being the most conservative bankers in their lending operations. Second, and more significant, the bankers "undoubtedly drew from [that] experience lessons that affected their future behavior. For both reasons, the banks that survived understandably placed far greater weight on liquidity than the banks in existence in 1929" (Friedman and Schwartz 1963: 449). Ironically, the whole experience of the 1929–1933 contraction made the surviving bankers even more skeptical of extending loans that would have taken the form of conventional real bills.

Unfortunately, the principal architects of monetary policy at the time did not have Friedman and Schwartz's work at their disposal. They did not consult measures of money stocks; nor would the remaining real bills advocates among them have given such measures any credence. To them, production came first, and the necessary money to finance it then followed—as long as the banks were on their toes. But with the banking system in tatters, no restorative mechanism was present. Fiscal spendthrifts, on the other hand, regarded the private sector as if it had been hypnotized or drugged. The only route they could see to economic recovery was for the government to "spend, spend, spend," as President Roosevelt put it in one of his fireside chats.

Virtually no one in the federal government of the mid-1930s was concerned with commercial banks' welfare or their optimal lending-and-investing operations. However, the banks' unprecedented holdings of excess legal reserves prompted a movement within the Fed, initiated by the Fed Bank of New York, to increase member bank reserve requirements in accordance with the provisions in the new Banking Act. Including such a provision in the act seemed, perhaps, to suggest its use.

At the time, reserve requirements were set at their minimum percentages, which would have allowed the member banks to more than double their total output of deposits, if at the same time they also doubled new loans and investments. (Balance sheets still had to balance.) However, nothing on the business horizon suggested that businesses or banks had much interest in any such real bills expansion at that time. Friedman and Schwartz (1963: 544) summarized the state of affairs:

> The rapid rise [in the stock of common money] was a consequence of the gold inflow produced by the revaluation of gold plus the flight of capital to the United States. It was in no way a consequence of the contemporaneous business expansion: the only way the expansion could significantly have increased the money stock would have been by inducing banks to hold smaller reserves, yet they were in fact doing the opposite.

That is, the banks wanted even more reserves than were available, even though they had significant excesses.

In spite of these conditions, and even though the economy was still depressed with about 18 percent unemployment, the Fed Board—prompted by the Fed Bank of New York, the secretary of the Treasury, and the opinions of money market pundits—raised member bank reserve requirements to their upper limits in three steps: in August 1936 by 50 percent, from 7, 10, and 13 percent for the various classes of banks, to 10.5, 15, and 19.5 percent; again in March 1937 by an additional 25 percent; and again in May 1937 by the final 25 percent that the law permitted.

Thus, by the end of June 1937, reserve requirements for the three classes of member banks were 14, 20, and 26 percent—double what they had been nine months earlier. The total increase "mopped up" all excess legal reserves. It was the equivalent of an open market sale of securities of approximately $3 billion. Since the 12 Fed banks at the time had only about $2.44 billion total government securities, the three reserve requirement increases had more monetary effect than would have occurred from the sale of all the securities in the Fed banks' portfolios (Friedman and Schwartz 1963: 526).

No one at the time seemed to realize just how artificial and harmful legal reserve requirements were to both the health and the stability of banking enterprise. To begin with, fixed legal reserve requirements cannot take account of all the diverse risks and uncertainties that dissimilar banks face, nor the varied conditions in which all the banks operate, nor how these different factors change over time.

Legal reserve requirements also interfere with the economical functioning of banks. Instead of a flexible cushion of reserves that banks can use in varying degree depending on the perceived risks of the moment, legal reserve requirements create a rigid line in the sand for bank lending. If a bank violates the line even briefly, it becomes subject to official penalties as well as to popular opprobrium for breaking the law. When no legal minimum ratios existed, which was the case in earlier banking eras, no law about them was there to be violated, so no popular anxiety could arise from any law being broken. A depositor who felt uncomfortable with his bank's management of its reserve position, would simply withdraw his deposits and redeposit them in a "safer" bank. Since bank managers were acutely aware of this possibility, they had every incentive to keep all the reserves necessary to support the loans they made.

Furthermore, better means are available to insure banker responsibility, such as imposing a double or triple liability penalty on bank owners' capital in the event of bank failure (Wood 2015: 94–95). This kind of constraint keeps bankers' heads clear and improves their concentration on banking principles. Significantly, the double liability penalty was prominent before the Banking Act of 1935 eliminated it (Friedman and Schwartz 1963: 447).

Most troubling of all, though, was the advertised reason for this unprecedented increase in legal reserve requirements: fear of inflation! The implicit contradiction is remarkable: the economy was still in the midst of the most severe depression in its history, but before all the mortgages had even been properly foreclosed, the monetary authorities in the political world—together with many financial analysts—were "worried" about possible inflation.

Benjamin M. Anderson, a conservative critic of New Deal policies and an unreconstructed real billser, observed that the great increases in bank reserves had had very little effect on interest rates. Therefore, mopping up legally excess reserves by raising reserve requirements would have very little effect in reverse, and would not compromise what he regarded as the limited effectiveness of monetary policy. Anderson's view also reflected the real bills notion that any monetary increase not inspired by a real bills loan was "inflationary," no matter what the state of the economy (Anderson [1949] 1980: 405).

A more realistic (political) reason for the increase was the competition for power between the Fed Board and Fed banks that the Banking Act of 1935 had aggravated. The Fed Board alone fixed reserve requirements. Once requirements were at their maximum percentages, the Fed's two other traditional policies—setting Fed bank discount rates and open-market operations in government securities—would become prominent again. The 12 Fed banks shared in determining these policies (Friedman and Schwartz 1963: 521–22).[1] Therefore, once reserve requirements were at their limits, regional Fed banks would have relatively more influence over policy.

Marriner Eccles, in his role as Fed chair, defended the first reserve requirement increase on technical grounds. The member banks' additional reserves arising from the newly monetized gold, he argued, "could become the basis of a potential expansion of bank credit of such proportions that the Federal Reserve could lose all control or influence over the supply and cost of money." Even though the Fed Board at this time saw no evidence of any "overexpansion of business activity," Eccles believed that an increase of at least 50 percent in reserve requirements was desirable. Reserves then would still "provide a more than adequate basis for legitimate credit expansion" (Eccles 1951: 291).

Although no one at the time saw fit to do so, Eccles's judgments on the adequacy of member banks' reserves can be subjected to a rather simple empirical analysis in a model using the quantity theory of money. The question neither Eccles nor anyone else asked, either at that time

---

[1] Friedman and Schwartz (1963) add several "technical" factors behind the decision to raise requirements.

or since, is this: How much money (*Mf*) would a fully employed U.S. economy, without inflation, require in 1936–1938, if simple and realistic assumptions are made to allow for growth in real output in proportion to growth in labor employment from 1929 on?[2] These figures could then be compared to the maximum quantity of money (*Mp*) the banks could have created in 1936–1937 under the new bank reserve requirements. If the *Mp* money stocks during the period were greater than the *Mf* money stocks, then some estimable amount of inflation could have occurred. However, as long as the *Mf* stocks were greater than computed maximum *Mp* stocks, no inflation would have been likely.

Table 4 collects money stocks, employment, and price level data into a time series that provides for a calculation of potential money stocks and employment for the relevant dates in order to estimate the likelihood of inflation or recession for this period. The paragraphs following the table describe the table in greater detail.

Columns 1, 2, and 3 record member bank deposits, member bank actual reserves, and member bank required reserves on the basis of the reserve ratios that the Fed Board applied at different times during the period.

Column 4, Excess Legal Reserves, is the computed excess of aggregate reserves over what Fed policy legally required on the same date.

Column 5, Potential Increase in Deposits, is a measure of how much Member Bank Deposits, Column 1, could have increased if the Excess Legal Reserves, Column 4, had been used for bank credit and deposit expansion in the same proportion that Required Reserves were currently being used. That is, Column 5 is simply a linear extrapolation of deposits based on the excess legal reserves of the moment, to measure the maximum deposits member banks could have generated. However, it does not provide for increases in currency holdings that would occur as the potential money stock grew. If it did, the values shown with an asterisk would be somewhat less. Additional holdings of hand-to-hand currency would detract from the bank reserves necessary to generate the banks' demand deposits.

---

[2] The necessary growth in jobs for a larger labor force does not speak to the growth in capital. Here the assumption is that the growth in capital would be complementary to the growth in the labor force.

TABLE 4

Selected Data for All Member Banks and the Potential Money Stock, 1935–1942 ($ billions)

DATE	MEMBER BANK DEPOSITS (1)	MEMBER BANK RESERVES (2)	MEMBER BANK REQUIRED RESERVES (3)	MEMBER BANKS' EXCESS LEGAL RESERVES (4)	POTENTIAL INCREASE IN DEPOSITS* (5)	MONEY STOCK ($M2$) (6)	POTENTIAL MONEY STOCK (MP) (7)	FULL EMPLOYMENT MONEY STOCK (MF) (8)	M2 EXCESS OR DEFICIENCY (%) ($MP/MF-1$) (9)	UNEMPLOYMENT (PERCENTAGE OF LABOR FORCE) (10)	PRICES (1947-1949=100) [NOTE: 1929=73.3] (11)
1935: June	27.4	5.39	2.95	2.44	22.7	38.1	60.8	57.7	5.4	20.1	58.7
–Dec. 31	28.9	6.28	3.3	2.98	26.1*	40.3	66.4*	59.2	12.2	18.5	59
1936: June	31.3	6.17	3.58	2.59	22.6*	43.3	65.9*	62.4	5.6	16.9	59.3
–Dec. 31	32.2	7.33	5.28	2.05	12.5	45	57.5	63.5	-9.5	15.6	60.3
1937: June	37.3	7.38	6.5	0.88	4.4	45.2	49.6	61.5	-19.3	14.3	61.4
–Dec. 31	31.7	7.71	6.64	1.07	5	44	49	61.6	-20.5	16.6	60.9
1938: June	31.6	8.61	5.85	2.76	14.9	44.1	59	64.4	-8.4	19	60.3
–Dec. 31	33.6	9.5	6.27	3.23	17.3	46.6	63.9	67.1	-4.8	18.1	59.9
1942: June	49.4	13.06	10.36	2.7	12.9	69	81.9	75.2	8.9	4.1	69.7

*Does not include increases in currency holdings that would occur as the potential money stock grew. If it did, the values shown with an asterisk would be somewhat less.
Sources: Cagan (1965: 350, Table F-8); Board of Governors (1943: 396–97); Friedman and Schwartz (1963: 714–15, Table A-1).

Column 6 shows actual money stocks, *M2*. This measure is the conventional one that includes deposits in all commercial banks, plus hand-to-hand currency outside of banks.

In Column 7, the maximum potential *M2* money stock is determined by the hypothetical increases in deposits from excess reserve expansion. It includes the data in Column 5 added to the actual money stock at each point in time, Column 6.

Column 8, the computed full-employment money stock, is the actual money stock, Column 6, but with two adjustments: (1) it includes the additional money that would have been necessary to accommodate the additional real output in goods and services that a fully employed labor force would have generated at the times noted, based on the actual unemployment data in Column 10, and (2) it includes the additional quantity of money that would have prompted prices to increase to their 1929 level. Prices in that year were at virtually the same level as in 1922. Money stock increases that brought prices back up to this level, therefore, should be considered only "reflationary," not inflationary.

To sum up, the simulation posits that computed full-employment money stocks (*Mf*, Column 8) at the various dates are actual money stocks (*M2*, Column 6) adjusted—that is, increased—to provide for the necessary increase in prices that would reflate the system to its 1929 price level. In addition, these computed money stocks must also be increased for the additional real output that would result from reemployment of currently unemployed labor.[3]

A comparison of Columns 7 and 8 in Table 4 shows that virtually any possibility of inflation at any point in this period was negligible. Between December 31, 1935, and June 30, 1936, the computed money stock maxima (Column 7) were slightly larger than the

[3] The quantity theory of money, $MV=PR$, is the basic model for computing these hypothetical money stocks. Money stocks, employment, and prices for June 1929 are the benchmark data. A full-employment money stock, Mf, for any subsequent date, is the actual money stock, Mt, for that date adjusted, first, by the ratio of the full-employment labor force to the number of workers actually employed on that date, Nf/Nt, and, second, by the ratio of the price index value of 1929 to the price index value of that date, Po/Pt. Then, the two money-stock-adjustments for prices and employment changes are added to the actual money stock values for that date to get the full employment-money-stock estimate. In mathematical terms,

$$Mf = Mt + [Nf/Nt \times Mt - Mt] + [(Po/Pt \times Mt) - Mt].$$

This expression reduces to

$$Mf = Mt [Nf/Nt + Po/Pt - 1].$$

full-employment money stocks (Column 8) on those dates, implying that some slight degree of inflation (Column 9) was possible. Thereafter, however, all the values turn negative, implying that the maximum money stocks that the commercial banking system could have created would never have reached full employment, let alone inflationary, levels. By December 31, 1937, the actual money stock (Column 6) had already started its decline, and recession was evident.

Several more inferences are possible from both Table 4 and anecdotal facts on the business environment:

First, the economy at this time suffered from an overwhelming dread of depression. The mood of a large majority of the people was that capitalism had failed and that a market system could neither guarantee "full employment" nor show any evidence that would lead anyone to expect it. Keynesian "animal spirits" and investment spending were almost nonexistent.

Second, the common presumption of "inflation" by Fed and Treasury officials, and the financial community, made no allowance for a time period of adjustment that would allow any volume of money-spending to reach full-employment values. The presumption of most observers was that the unprecedented levels of excess reserves could generate inflation the next day.

Third, no one, either before or since, observed that some significant quantity of the calculated excess reserves would, in the event of a general monetary increase, be used as hand-to-hand currency. That is, when the economy's money stock expanded over time, the currency–deposit ratio, which had not been repealed, would result in some portion of the existing bank reserves being converted into currency. This gradual conversion to currency in the presence of an expanding quantity of bank deposits would reduce the total amount of reserves available for the new deposits and significantly reduce the total amount of deposit money that could otherwise have been created. It would, therefore, have reduced the potential money stock values (Column 7) by a measurable amount.[4]

---

[4] As the total stock of money expanded in the mid-1930s and before 1937, the currency–deposit ratio actually declined, as would be expected during the partial recovery. Nonetheless, if a complete

Fourth, and most important, no one at the time looked at the actual "excess" reserves the banks held and comprehended that, to the bankers who were actually operating the banks, these reserves were necessary, no matter what the legal requirements were.

Legal reserve requirements were bureaucratic constructions, without any empirical investigation into the percentages of reserves that bankers thought they needed. Simply because the banks could legally have expanded loans and deposits but were not doing so did not by any stretch of logic mean that the reserves labeled "excess" were redundant. To the bankers they were very much required. The Fed-Treasury doubling of legal reserve requirements to the maximum value the law allowed, spooked bankers into increasing the reserve percentages they required to something more than what had satisfied them earlier. They had maintained 14, 20, and 26 percent when legal requirements were 7, 10, and 13 percent. Now, legal requirements had been increased enough to eliminate all these desired reserve cushions. The bankers could see no reason for such a policy. It increased their uncertainties about the future course of Fed policy. They now wanted even more reserves than the "excess" they previously had. "Mopping up" was not in their lexicon.[5]

The most amazing feature of the reserve requirement episode has been that virtually no one, except for Friedman and Schwartz (1963: 506–45), believed it had anything to do with the severe recession of 1937–1938. Fed Chair Eccles, who had, to his credit, argued against the final 50 percent increase, still could not comprehend properly the quantity of money that the system needed. He argued in retrospect that by November 1936 total bank deposits and currency were at

---

income-spending pattern had developed toward a full-employment value, some additional currency would have been diverted from the banks' excess reserves and would have retarded in part the expansion of deposits.

[5] Demands for excess reserves determine a relationship $r^*=(1+d)r$ between bankers' desired reserve/deposit ratio r^* and the minimum legally required ratio r. Here d is a parameter representing banker distrust of the Fed. Ordinarily, d is zero, as when the Fed fulfills its duty as lender of last resort (LLR). In this case, desired and required reserve ratios coincide. But when, as in the early 1930s, the Fed fails in its LLR responsibilities, d takes on a value greater than zero. In this case, bankers wish to hold excess reserves as a precaution against inability to obtain emergency liquidity from the Fed. Accordingly, the desired reserve ratio becomes larger than the required one. And such happens even when, as in 1936–1937, the latter ratio is doubled.

higher levels than they had been in 1929 and therefore were sufficient for a recovery (Eccles 1951: 290).[6]

What Eccles, and most other observers, did not take into account was the large increase in employable resources—employable labor and capital—that had come into existence in the seven years since 1929. Eccles did note correctly that the velocity of money had fallen. "If money [total bank deposits and hand-to-hand currency] were utilized at a rate of turnover comparable to pre-depression levels," he observed, "they would be sufficient to sustain a vastly greater level of business activity" (Eccles 1951: 270). While this is true, a complete analysis using the quantity theory of money would have suggested that the velocity of money always falls in a severe recession or depression and increases during recoveries. Nonetheless, even if the velocity of money had regained its 1929 buoyancy, another significant increase in money was needed to accommodate what would have been the increase in output from a fully employed economy.[7] The practical consequences of these two variables over the period 1929–1937 are what Table 4 records.

The doubling of reserve requirements as a monetary policy device was a novel experiment for Fed-Treasury policymakers. Since the increase in requirements still allowed the banking system to retain the volume of existing deposits, many observers of monetary affairs, from the late 1930s to the present, have argued that the reserve requirement increases did not contribute significantly to the recession of 1937. Even though the Fed Board doubled requirements, the commercial banks still had the legally required reserves on their books. Member banks could satisfy the doubling of requirements simply by accounting all existing reserves as "required" instead of accounting half as "excess." This arithmetic, however, does not reach the dynamics of the extraordinary reserve requirement increase. By this time, as Friedman and Schwartz (1963) noted, commercial bankers were "shell-shocked."

[6] Actually, *M1* was slightly higher ($30.4 billion compared with $26.7 billion in 1929), but *M2* was lower ($44.4 billion compared with $46.4 billion in 1929).

[7] Table 4 shows that a fully employed economy would have needed $63.5 billion in December 1936 when it had only $45.0 billion. The increase in the quantity of money necessary to restore the 1929 price level implicitly accounts and compensates for changes in velocity.

The economy in early 1937 was still only at about 75 percent of capacity (i.e., full employment). Bankers clearly wanted a significant positive difference between their actual dollar reserves and the required dollar reserves computed from the Fed's legal reserve requirement.

Besides the still-deficient financial activity, however, other uglier implications seem reasonable. First, the very fact that a reserve requirement increase occurred at all implied that policymakers wanted less enthusiastic business (and banking) activity, even though no real recovery had yet taken hold. If that was not the case, then why have any increase at all, especially one of this magnitude?

Second, the effect of the announcement of the reserve requirement increases on bankers, who had just witnessed the worst business depression in history, added significantly to the recession mode that was pending. No banker could imagine any reason for any increase in reserve requirements at the time. Thus the announcement "spooked" bankers into an even more conservative attitude toward any new lending activity. Notably, no reserve requirement policy changes since then have approached the magnitude of those in 1936–1937. So, yes, the blundering reserve requirement increases triggered the new recession in spite of the seemingly benign arithmetic of Fed-Treasury policy.

Bad as the reserve requirement increases were, however, the Fed-Treasury policies that resulted in the recession of 1937 were not to be the end of the story. Waiting in the wings to make matters worse was Secretary of the Treasury Henry Morgenthau, who had a plan to neutralize even further the incoming stocks of gold that would have supplied monetary relief.

(15)

TREASURY GOLD POLICY
AND THE 1937–1938 RECESSION

The devaluation of the gold dollar in 1934, together with the U.S. Treasury's "profit" from this expropriation, had provided the Treasury with a $2 billion cash balance to be used primarily for exchange rate controls. The Treasury thus had a gold "position" in the world, which also gave it the means to influence gold policy for any purpose it felt important.

The banks' accumulation of excess reserves had attracted the attention of all policymakers, including Henry Morgenthau, the secretary of the Treasury. Morgenthau sensed a role for the Treasury that would also further the Fed Board's move to maximize reserve requirements. As previously explained, all gold that came into the country had to go through the U.S. Treasury, where it was duly monetized into gold certificates. And lots of gold was still coming in, both because of the gold devaluation and because of political uncertainties in Europe.

Morgenthau decided to "help" the Fed Board control the incipient "inflation." Beginning December 22, 1936, after the Fed Board's first 50 percent increase in reserve requirements—which of course precluded any possibility of inflation—Morgenthau had all incoming gold placed in an "inactive" account. Instead of paying the Fed for the gold with new $100,000 gold certificates, the Treasury sold government securities in the open market to offset (and negate) what would have been an increase in bank reserves—a move that was decidedly deflationary and of dubious legality.[1] As a result of his action, all incoming gold was stockpiled in the Treasury without being monetized (Friedman and Schwartz 1963: 510–11). The Treasury Department

---

[1] The new Banking Act placed the authority to make open market sales or purchases in the province of the Federal Open Market Committee.

effectively became the central bank during this episode, and its monetary policy was very depressive—as, indeed, was the intention.

By February 1937 the actual money stock, $M2$, was \$45.0 billion; the potential money stock had been reduced to \$57.5 billion because of the first reserve requirement increase; and the computed full-employment money stock was well out of reach at \$63.5 billion (see Table 4). Whatever chance the economy might have had to recover to a position near full employment disappeared entirely. The Treasury's deflationary gold policy and the Federal Reserve's further increases in reserve requirements in March and May 1937 ordained a severe recession. By June 30, 1937, nothing of the budding recovery was left. The potential money stock was now \$19 billion below its full-employment value, and prices had started to decline.

The developing recession convinced Morgenthau that perhaps the danger of inflation was past. In September 1937 he authorized the release of \$300 million of the more than \$1 billion of gold that had been sequestered, thereby restarting the machinery of gold monetization. Finally, in April 1938, he announced abandonment of the deflationary gold policy altogether.

The Treasury's gold policy lasted 16 months—December 1936 to April 1938. The Fed's reserve requirement policy started in August 1936, but while it ended in May 1937, its effect was enduring: no compensating reduction of requirements came before 1942. Both policies were significantly deflationary, as our analysis, Alan Meltzer's *A History of the Federal Reserve*, and Friedman and Schwartz's *Monetary History* confirm.[2]

Friedman and Schwartz (1963: 524) also note that, aside from Marriner Eccles, no official policymaker in the Fed or Treasury gave any

consideration [to] the total stock of money as a magnitude that either was or should be controlled by the System, nor of changes

---

[2] See Friedman and Schwartz (1963: 459–83, 506–45). Their detailed account of the monetary developments of this era and their analysis of the events during the period 1929–1938 are incomparable and definitive. See also Meltzer (2003: 490–530).

in the stock as measuring the impact of the System. The System's role was seen exclusively in terms of conditions [interest rates] in the money market, i.e., the market for loans and investments.

The blunder of ignoring the quantity of money, and any significant changes in it, was only too apparent. By neglecting to use the quantity theory of money as a means for analyzing policy, Federal Reserve and Treasury "fiscalists" vastly underestimated the effects of both the increases in reserve requirements and the gold sterilization policy.

Friedman and Schwartz discuss at length the new prominence of fiscal policy: this change grew out of the view that "money does not matter," which in turn resulted from the ". . . widely accepted [opinion] that monetary measures had been found wanting in the twenties and the early thirties. . . . Emphasis shifted to fiscal measures. . . . Deficit spending, pump priming, and public works—not central bank policies—were widely regarded as the means to recovery" (Friedman and Schwartz 1963: 533).[3] They also observe that this policy could not have been "Keynesian" because the Keynesian doctrine had not yet had time to appear. It was just seat-of-the-pants fiscalism. Thus, two monetary doctrines were prominent by the mid-1930s: the Real Bills Doctrine, however unrecognized and in decline, and the new Treasury fiscalism. The Federal Reserve System had changed from a real bills Federal Reserve System to a fiscal policy central bank. It would remain in that state indefinitely.[4]

Treasury-dominated Federal Reserve policies, far from being roundly condemned by economists and the financial press at the time, were enthusiastically endorsed. "Even the extraordinary increases in reserve requirements," wrote economist G. Griffith Johnson, "would have been insufficient to bring excess reserves [down] to reasonable size if it had not been for the cooperation of the Treasury through the

[3] In general, Friedman and Schwartz (1963: 497) support our view: "The broad movements in the stock of money correspond with those in income."

[4] Fed policy in the coming decades had several catchy names: "bills only," "bills usually," and even "monetarism"—which Federal Reserve spokesmen proclaimed "did not work." However, the Federal Reserve's "monetarism" was anything but *true* monetarism. It was, rather, an excuse for monetarism that was designed not to work. Never did Federal Reserve policy try to gainsay Treasury policy. For a full account of that statement, see Friedman and Schwartz (1963: 620–38).

gold sterilization program. . . . One may be skeptical of the wisdom with which monetary instruments will be used, but . . . [it] is a risk which must be assumed under a democratic or any other form of government" (Johnson 1939: 218, 223).

But is it? Under a true gold standard, as implied by the U.S. Constitution, the Treasury would not have had a "gold policy." The gold standard, which was still formally on the books when Johnson wrote, was *the* policy and was self-regulating. Gold would not have been stockpiled in the Treasury, but would have been in commercial banks and, by this time, in foreign monetary systems where it would have served its formal function of securing bank deposits and bank-issued currency under the constraint of convertibility. Such systems would also have included real bills lending and creation of deposits and currency. However, the Real Bills Doctrine would not have had the opportunity to become the organizing principle of the entire monetary system, as it did in 1929, and overwhelm the stabilizing effects of the constitutional gold standard.

Virtually all economists, whether they thought Fed policies wise or foolish, agreed that monetary policy had to be man-made and coordinated with Treasury fiscal policy. Johnson claimed that Congress had given over the Fed's powers of monetary control to the executive branch of government because monetary policy had proved ineffective. Consequently, these powers had become more "democratic" because "they were now exercised by politically responsible officials . . . and would eventually be subject to review by the electorate." "In large part," Johnson concluded, "the [Federal Reserve] System has served as a technical instrument for effecting the Treasury's policies" (Johnson 1939: 205–11). Johnson spared himself the impossible task of showing how "the electorate" would be able to "review" monetary policy—or have any effect on it.

Other mainstream economists commented on the politicization of the Fed. "The Federal Reserve Board," stated Frederick Bradford, in a paper read before the American Economic Association, "although ostensibly independent, has . . . come practically under political domination" (Bradford 1935: 672).

Another prominent economist, John H. Williams (cited in Chapter 9) initiated the notion that the Fed should be at "arm's length" from the government—that it should be "governmental" without being "political." He applauded the change in control from the diffused Fed banks to the centralized Board of Governors. "How the System will function," he wrote, "will depend more on [the System's] personnel, their understanding and judgment, than upon specific legislative provisions" (Williams 1936: 156–57). For a "government of laws," such a view of governmental activity is contradictory

The equally well-regarded economist, Jacob Viner of the University of Chicago (also cited in Chapter 9) noted the prominence of personalities in the revised Federal Reserve System. "The relative strength of personalities," rather than "the legal definition of lines of authority," would determine the path for monetary policy. "Harmonization of the two sets of authorities," he said, "must be through exchange of views between agencies that meet as equals rather than making one agency the mere instrumentality of the other." Further on, his view of "agencies which meet as equals" vanished when he discussed the possibility of a monetary rule for the Fed to follow. The agencies in fact were not "equal," and the Fed should face no specific mandate for policy, he concluded, because it had to adjust its activities to those of the Treasury, which "has credit control [interest rate] powers . . . co-ordinate with its own, and [is] pursuing objectives which are avowedly extemporized from day to day" (Viner 1936: 106–16.).

All these comments from economists reflect three things: First, no working gold standard was functioning. Rather, gold stocks were being managed by the U.S. Treasury; and both gold monetization and ownership by any private institutions were prohibited. Second, since money did not matter, except for its effect on interest rates, monetary policy became very much subject to Treasury control in its effort to float government loans at favorable rates. Finally, the Real Bills Doctrine, although still present, no longer decisively influenced monetary policy. Many economists and some policymakers still cherished it, but the new fiscalism paid it no heed.

16

CONCLUSION: THREE MONETARY STANDARDS AND THE FEDERAL RESERVE

Milton Friedman liked to recall that his experience with the Great Depression as a young man living in New York had a major effect on his decision to study economics. So, we can count at least one good thing that came out of that tragic decade. His and Anna Schwartz's epic account of the Great Contraction (1929–1933) in their *Monetary History* tells most of what happened during that unhappy time. Their study is empirical and analytic economics at its best. Those of us who are following in their footsteps have had this superb model of economic research and exposition to guide our further research on that worrisome and, at times, puzzling event.

Despite the evidence in *A Monetary History* and its superb documentation of events and institutions, seriously flawed treatments of events and institutions are still prominent in professional economic accounts of the 10 to 12 years of the Great Depression. The research we have brought to bear here is meant to correct those errors. Our investigation has emphasized two monetary institutions for supplying the U.S. economy with money—the gold standard and the Federal Reserve System—and three doctrines or theories that the latter institution has featured when operational: the Real Bills Doctrine, the quantity theory of money, and Treasury-fiscalist-spending theory, which demotes the Fed to nothing more than a supporting agency for the spending policies of the Treasury. Our primary focus is on the Real Bills Doctrine. We have emphasized its relationship to the gold standard, its place in monetary theory, and how one of its postulates—anti-speculation policy—came to dominate Federal Reserve policy in the United States during the early 1930s. The destruction of gold money and the gold standard followed. Then the Banking Act of 1935 and the reserve requirement recession of 1937–1938 completed the extraordinary monetary experiences of the time.

The Real Bills Doctrine grew out of the gold standard. Bankers faced constant criticism for their creation of bank currency and bank deposits while operating commercial banks with only fractional gold reserves. They responded that the real bills they acquired from lending, by their very nature—short-term, self-liquidating loans with real goods as collateral—were *almost as good* as gold. Indeed, so long as a bank was judicious and conservative in its lending policies, it had no trouble redeeming its demand obligations with gold or other legal tender, and the real bills argument was not violated.

Several milestones marked the doctrine's evolution from its gold origins. First came the notion that desirable near-constancy of the price level might be achieved if the money stock varied one-for-one with the final real output it purchased. Next came the idea that this goal might best be accomplished by having real output itself generate the very money required to buy it off the market at prevailing prices. There followed the realization that output could indeed drive the money stock if banks, which created banknotes and checking deposits by way of loans, would lend only against collateral arising from real goods in the process of production. Then came the suggestion that the particular asset, land, might serve as the proxy collateral for real output. Finally, the Real Bills Doctrine emerged fully formed when land gave way to commercial paper as the asset best representing real output.

Critics noted that crucial errors had entered the doctrine, marring its use as a monetary rule. For one thing, the doctrine's formulators tied the nominal money stock not to the physical quantity of goods, as they had intended to do, but rather to the nominal dollar volume of commercial paper emanating from the dollar value of that output. By tying one nominal variable, the money stock, to another nominal variable—the dollar volume of commercial paper that moves in step with prices—the doctrine created a potentially destabilizing feedback loop. Prices and money, once disturbed, could chase each other upward or downward indefinitely in a vicious inflationary or deflationary spiral. True, there were some ways to avert this development, but they all involved supplementing the real bills mechanism with non–real bills monetary constraints, particularly some kind of control over the economy's stock of money.

The doctrine's second flaw was that its implementation could cause the money stock to vary pro-cyclically with nominal (and real) activity, rather than countercyclically as a stabilizing monetary policy would do. Far from damping down business cycles, the doctrine could prolong them when and if its operations coincided with anticipation of higher or lower prices. By itself, the doctrine did not encourage instability if the business environment was stable. But once some unseemly financial event occurred—such as an impossible reparations mandate, a policy of pegging loan interest rates above or below their natural equilibrium levels, or a moralistic fervor against speculation—the Real Bills Doctrine supported an unstable disequilibrium in the financial-monetary system. Most important here, when the doctrine opposed loans made for "speculative" as distinct from "productive" purposes in 1929–1930 as if they were mutually exclusive, it set in motion a financial disaster that lasted 10 years. First, it failed to take into account that all production, because of the uncertainty of its future profitability, *must* include a speculative element. Second, speculative activity, to the extent that it helps create real value, is fundamentally productive.[1] For these two reasons, the alleged distinction between production and speculation is, to a very large degree, a false dichotomy.

The Federal Reserve Act that Congress passed in 1913 included some real bills principles, but it did not specifically make the Fed a real bills central bank. Rather, the regional Fed banks were to be private banks that would take over the emergency functions initiated by the clearinghouse associations and make them "legitimate." The Fed was cast as an eclectic institutional mix of credit supplementation

---

[1] We have not seen this thesis developed professionally. We suggest that this lack should encourage critical treatment, especially since "speculation" has had such sinful implications and explications in the past.

for commercial member banks operating under a gold standard. Fed banks were supposed to follow real bills precepts in making loans, but the gold standard was still the only legitimate basis for the functioning of any banking and monetary system. This ultimate primacy of the gold standard was affirmed in the Currency Act of 1900 and in the Federal Reserve Act of 1913 as well.

A myth that remains popular today is that the gold standard was the behind-the-scenes villain that promoted the Great Contraction and all the other economic problems that followed in the 1930s. This contention is clearly mistaken. The *operational* gold standard ended forever at the time the United States became a belligerent in World War I. From 1917 on, the movements of gold into and out of the United States no longer even approximately determined the economy's stock of common money.

The contention that Federal Reserve policymakers were "managing" the gold standard is an oxymoron—a contradiction in terms. A "gold standard" that is "managed" is not and cannot be a true gold standard. It is a standard of whoever is doing the managing. Furthermore, without regard to whether gold was managed or not, the original Federal Reserve Act gave the Fed Board complete statutory power to abrogate all the reserve requirement restrictions on gold that the act specified for Federal Reserve banks (Board of Governors 1961: 34–35). If the Board had used these clearly stated powers any time after 1929, the Fed banks could have stopped the contraction in its tracks, even if doing so exhausted their gold reserves entirely.

After World War I, the New York Fed, under the guidance of Benjamin Strong and in the absence of a working gold standard, initiated a policy of price level stabilization. The New York Fed was in the right financial environment to implement this policy; the postwar U.S. economy after the 1920–1922 recession was the right time to begin it; and Benjamin Strong was the right man to run this showcase model of central bank policy. It lasted from 1922 until late 1928, when Strong died of tuberculosis (Chandler 1958: 194–206).[2] The policy implied

---

[2] In fact, the policy had some momentum and did not end until mid-1929. See also Friedman and Schwartz (1963: 251, 411–15).

that the Fed had become a quantity theory of money quasi–central bank, with a dormant gold standard waiting in the wings.

With Strong's death, a scramble began for control of the monetary machinery. Friedman and Schwartz's *A Monetary History* provides much documentary evidence on the personalities on the Federal Reserve Board and in the Fed banks, vying for control, and on the critical policy decisions that occurred. Then came perdition! If the Fed could be a stable price level central bank without a viable gold standard, then surely it could eschew the quantity theory of money and become a real bills central bank—still without a viable gold standard. Indeed, the Federal Reserve Act included sections that suggested such an institution (Board of Governors 1961: 43–51).

The act did not sanction the onslaught against "speculation" that followed. But the supporters of the Real Bills Doctrine, who gained control of the Federal Reserve in 1929, treated any bank lending for stock market "gambling" as a vice on a par with the stable price level policy of Benjamin Strong and the New York Fed, which they had repeatedly condemned. Hence, they stopped "speculation" by a policy of "direct pressure" on commercial bank lending and in so doing unleashed an avalanche of bank failures much beyond anything preceding it in the history of banking.

The mistakes of the real bills Fed did not stop there. Fed spokesmen and others were able to deflect blame for the cataclysm of the Great Contraction to an alleged ineffectiveness of the gold standard for not providing a stabilizing counterforce to the ongoing liquidations. This contention, however, only shows that the gold standard was obviously not functioning. It had been inoperative since 1914, when the federal government took over control of banking and the securities market to provide expedient financing for World War I. To blame the gold standard for the Great Depression was clearly wrong. In any case, proponents of the Real Bills Doctrine, while in control of the Fed, paid only lip service to the gold standard—and not much of that. Speculation, not "the" gold standard, was their whipping boy.

Leland Yeager (1966: 290) describes the "gold standard" of the 1920s in these words:

> The gold standard of the late 1920s was hardly more than a façade. It involved extreme measures to economize gold . . . [including] the neutralization or offsetting of international influences on domestic money supplies, incomes, and prices. Gold standard methods of balance-of-payments equilibrium were largely destroyed and were not replaced by any alternative. . . . With both the price-and-income and the exchange-rate mechanisms of balance-of-payments adjustment out of operation, disequilibriums were accumulated or merely palliated, not continuously corrected.

Friedman and Schwartz (1963: 474) also comment that "whatever the monetary system was in the early 'thirties, it was not a gold standard."

The war on gold followed the Fed's successful evasion of culpability for the Great Contraction. Combined with the popular view of the time that monetary policy itself was ineffective, this war on gold witnessed the final destruction of the gold standard as a money-determining institution.

The gold standard has now been nonoperational for over a century. Despite its many qualities—its constitutionalism, its disciplined determination of the money stock, and its constraining effect on government overreach—its undeserved culpability for the Great Depression and its prickly discipline in fiscal affairs prevent its political acceptance as a national policy. The Federal Reserve–Treasury system is, and will continue to be for the foreseeable future, the primary agent of control over the monetary system.

With the demise of the gold standard, the Real Bills Doctrine was soon stripped of its lamentable role as the guiding principle of monetary policy. Treasury–Federal Reserve central banks do not need a Real Bills Doctrine to excuse or guide their policies. They manage commercial banks' reserves without reference to either gold or real bills.

The present-day Fed creates two forms of money—commercial-member bank reserve accounts and Federal Reserve notes. Both may serve as bank reserves, but only the notes serve as hand-to-hand currency.[3] Commercial banks, using the reserves and currency that the Fed creates, then provide checkbook deposits for their clientele by making loans to businessmen and other borrowers. Since the Fed creates almost all the money that the economy uses, it is naturally a quantity theory of money central bank, even if Fed managers do not mention the quantity theory when devising actual monetary policy.[4] They often use some important interest rate, such as the Fed funds rate, in their policy reports. Nonetheless, the Fed's power to create and destroy the economy's stock of money is profound and unequivocal. To create the right quantity of money, however, the Fed must be politically constrained by some means. The gold standard without the Fed was such a means: the limited quantity of gold in the earth's crust rationed the quantity of gold and, therefore, all other money.

No contemporary central bank faces any "natural" check on its money-supplying powers, so some other device or political rule must be applied to constrain it. If the velocity of money is a near constant, the obvious "best" rule is to tie the growth in the money stock to the growth in the economy's real output. Both the quantity theory and the Real Bills Doctrine, properly formulated, imply this rule. However, the velocity of money can be very inconstant, particularly in periods like the present and recent past, when numerous financial innovations change it in unexpected ways. Given the frequent shifts in measured velocity, tying the money stock to the rate of growth in the economy's total annual product cannot be an effective stabilization policy.

The optimal alternative is to obtain constancy in an average of money prices, as measured by a reliable price index that captures the influence of velocity as well as the growth in real output on money prices. That is the only effective policy that provides a high degree of constancy to the value of the unit of account—here, the dollar. True,

---

[3] The U.S. Treasury furnishes a relatively small amount of hand-to-hand coin-currency.

[4] The executive branch through the Treasury often dominates Federal Reserve policies. However, as a technical matter, the Fed creates all but the small amount of fractional currency that the economy uses. The following analysis discusses how monetary policy would have to be conducted absent any executive or congressional pressures.

the index would lag some actual money price movements by a short time interval, so the next (short) period's policy would be based on the last period's prices. In practice, however, this divergence would not be important.[5]

The signal for the Fed to undertake monetary change should not be "interest rates," either short term or long term. The Fed does not, and cannot, permanently "control interest rates." Real interest rates are determined by real factors—investors' "animal spirits," their anticipation of provident real returns on the investments they make, and the willingness of savers not to consume all their incomes. However, the Fed does control the quantity of money in the economy, and it may increase that quantity by buying government securities in the open market, which also has the effect of reducing nominal interest rates. Politicians and pundits then exclaim that "The Fed has lowered interest rates." Though a few short-term interest rates may temporarily decline, and business and industry may experience a temporary blip upward, the Fed's action has changed only the economy's quantity of money. This increase can easily be managed so that it is just enough to market new output with little or no change in the average of prices.

A very large fraction of laypeople, however, do not understand the mechanics of monetary change—how it is generated by both commercial banks and the central bank. They do understand a decrease, or a "hike," in interest rates, because they borrow money at the bank to buy a home or a car; and the lower or higher the rates they pay, the more or less house or car they can buy. Take away the central bank's power to control the quantity of base and common money, however, and its power to raise or lower interest rates disappears.

Since the money-creating Federal Reserve–Treasury system will be in control of monetary-fiscal policy for the indefinite future, the problem of constraining it to some sort of constitutional limitation by an explicit rule is crucial (see Dorn 2018). Otherwise, the discretion of the Fed's Open Market Committee with all its human failings will prevail. Monetary policymaking experience through the last

---

[5] Governor Benjamin Strong of the New York Fed proved the efficacy of this principle from 1922 to 1929. It would still be an excellent principle for today's Fed to follow.

century, and all the evidence in this book, confirm that human discretion over control of the money stock, no matter how heavenly it
could be if policymakers were angels, will continue to be less than
ideal because policymakers are self-serving humans.

Thus, the monetary system must have a constraining rule to ensure
monetary stability. The gold standard was such a rule—and it endured
in one form or another for centuries. Then, Benjamin Strong's policy
of primitive price level stabilization, while not explicitly a rule, nevertheless approximated one inasmuch as it promoted rules-like behavior
in the economy's price level. Under both systems the U.S. economy, as
well as most of the world's economies, prospered.

Otherwise, the only way to neutralize the activities of the central
bank is to take the control of money completely out of the hands of the
FOMC. To implement such a policy, Congress would have to freeze
the monetary base—the sum of Federal Reserve–created money,
which includes outstanding Federal Reserve notes (currency) and
the reserve-deposit accounts of all member banks in Federal Reserve
banks. While this policy has merit, it is neither as understandable, nor
popularly acceptable as a stable price level rule or a gold standard. The
latter is now practically out of the question, despite its proven efficacy
when its operation is left to the market system. Fortunately, the stable
price level rule has similar operational features, it is technically easy to
implement, and it lacks the century-old prejudice that has been built
into the gold standard. Hence, we recommend a stable price level rule
to constrain the Fed and the government that operates it. We will leave
the gold standard to some distant future era when the government's
stock of gold has been redistributed and can again become a viable
monetary base.[6]

---

[6] That stock at present is approximately 8,125 tons, held in Ft. Knox and other depositaries.

Appendix:
A Simple Schema of the Real Bills Doctrine

The Real Bills Doctrine says that as long as banks lend only against sound, short-term, self-liquidating commercial paper issued to finance real goods in the process of production, the money stock will automatically vary with and be just sufficient to purchase, at prevailing prices, those goods when they reach the market as finished product. It is a rule claiming to synchronize real output with its own means of purchase and with the volume of bank credit used to finance production.

Surprisingly, the doctrine's proponents never bothered to bolster their contention—that a real bills–based money stock will be just sufficient to accommodate and purchase the economy's real output at existing prices—with a succinct formal symbolic derivation. Clarity and precision render it useful to do so here.

First, define the needs of trade N as the value of inventories of working capital, or goods-in-process G—the production and marketing of which is financed by bank loans. Symbolically,

(1) $N = G$.

Second, assume that each dollar's worth of goods-in-process G generates an equivalent quantity of paper claims in the form of commercial bills B, which business borrowers offer as collateral to back their demand for bank loans L_D to finance real production. That is, assume that

(2) $G = B$,

and that

(3) $B = L_D$.

Here it is crucial to stress that the bills, B, variable is strictly defined to include only short-term commercial paper deriving from private real production. All other forms of paper, such as that financing consumer, home mortgage, real estate, government, long-term capital investment, and stock market loans, for example, are ruled out as representing nonproductive activity. Eligible paper consists solely of short-term commercial paper arising from, and therefore securing, real production—and nothing else.

Third, the foregoing loan demands L_D pass the real bills test—that is, they are secured by claims to real goods in the process of production—and therefore qualify for matching supplies of bank loans L_S at some interest rate as indicated by the expression

(4) $L_D = L_S$.

Fourth, since banks supply loans to borrowers in the form of banknotes and checking deposits, the sum of which composes the stock of bank money, the dollar value of loans L_S equals that of money stock M,

(5) $L_S = M$.

Substituting equations (1) through (4) into (5) and solving for the money stock yields

(6) $M = N$,

which says that, as long as banks lend only against short-term commercial bills arising from transactions in real goods and services, the stock of bank money M will match the needs of trade, N. But since the needs of trade N is by definition the same as the value of goods-in-process G, one can also write

(7) $M = G$,

which states that the supply of bank money M is ultimately secured by goods-in-process G. This condition ensures that when those goods reach the market as finished product they will be matched by just enough money to purchase them at prevailing prices. This result—that the money stock is just sufficient to buy the goods produced—can be shown by defining the value of goods-in-process G as the product of the price P and quantity Q of those goods when they emerge in the form of final output. That is,

(8) $G = PQ.$

Equation (8) avoids a stock-flow problem by treating the inventory of goods-in-process G, a *stock of working capital existing at a point of time*, as turning over once per period in the production of final output Q, a *flow of goods measured over an interval of time*. In this case, we multiply the goods-in-process G variable by its implied turnover of 1. This operation converts G from a stock into a flow, thus rendering both sides of the equation dimensionally equivalent.

Substituting equations (8) and (5) into (7) yields

(9) $M = L_S = PQ,$

which says that taking prices P as given and determined by nonmonetary considerations, the money stock M and volume of bank credit L_S vary in step with real production Q.

Note that equation (9) is simply the well-known equation of exchange $MV = PQ$ with money's rate of use, or circulation velocity V, assigned a value of one, or unity. The unit velocity term corresponds to the real bills notion of the self-liquidating loan according to which output induces, via collateralized loans, money just sufficient to purchase it and then to retire the loans. Buyers spend the money once and once only on the final product such that $V = 1$. Recipient producers then use the resulting sales receipts to pay off their loans, and the money returns to the banks, which retire it from circulation. (The doctrine's critics had a field day with this assertion, noting that money, once created, might be spent several times before loans were repaid. Even when loans were repaid, bankers could relend the proceeds so that the new money would remain in circulation with a velocity greater than unity.)

Two last equations complete the model. Together they explain the passive, reserve-granting rediscount function of the central bank in fractional-reserve real bills banking systems. Banks, facing a mandatory legal reserve ratio r, must possess the reserves R necessary to back the money M and credit dictated by the needs of trade. The central bank may enable them to do so by rediscounting the commercial paper, or real bills, they have acquired from their customers. By limiting the type of paper eligible for rediscount, a proper central bank ensures that reserves are just sufficient to underwrite production. In an ideal real bills regime uncomplicated by gold convertibility and cash flows, the central bank's discount window passively supplies all reserves necessary to meet the needs of trade. It does so at discount rates normally set below short-term market interest rates so as to pose no barrier to accommodation.

In short, the banking system faces a reserve constraint

$$(10)\ R = rM,$$

which it satisfies by borrowing reserves from the central bank. With nonborrowed reserves ignored, all reserves R are borrowed reserves R_B such that

$$(11)\ R = R_B.$$

Here is the real bills view of the central bank as passive accommodator rather than active initiator of changes in economic activity. Causation runs from output and prices to loans and thence to bank money, with the central bank supplying the necessary reserves. Standing at the end of the causal queue, the central bank never forces money on the economy. It merely supplies reserves passively on demand. Of course, it might influence this demand through changes in its rediscount rate. In such a case, borrowed reserves would become an inverse function of the discount rate d and equation (11) would be expressed as $R = R_B(d)$. Even so, the central bank still would accept all real bills tendered it at the prevailing rate, especially if the discount rate was set at or below market rates so as not to discourage borrowing. The passive, accommodating function of the discount window could not be clearer.

Equations (1) through (11) constitute the essence of the Real Bills Doctrine. Two main shortcomings of the doctrine are immediately apparent from equation (9), which treats causation as running from nominal business activity to money rather than vice versa. Shortcoming number one is that the doctrine has money behaving in a perversely destabilizing pro-cyclical manner rather than in a stabilizing countercyclical one. According to the equation, positive shocks to nominal national income PQ that precipitate inflationary booms also trigger money stock increases that support, underwrite, and amplify those booms. Likewise, negative shocks to PQ that put the economy on a deflationary path induce money stock contractions that prolong the downturn. This state of affairs is exactly the opposite the way stabilizing countercyclical monetary policy is supposed to work. By having money move with the cycle rather than against it, the doctrine increases the amplitude and lengthens the duration of cyclical swings rather than damping and shortening them. On this ground alone, the doctrine fails as a stabilization rule.

A second and even more damaging shortcoming is the doctrine's confusion of nominal with real magnitudes as shown in equation (9). That equation links money not to real physical output Q but rather to the nominal dollar price-times-quantity value PQ of that output. By anchoring each dollar of money to a dollar's worth of goods, the doctrine sets up a dynamically unstable price-money-price feedback loop whose elements are free to expand or contract without limit.

It is easy to spot the doctrine's fundamental fallacy: to treat real product Q as money's sole governor, the doctrine must take prices P as given and fixed. In fact, however, those prices move directly under the impact of the money stock itself. Advocates of the Real Bills Doctrine failed to perceive this two-way inflationary interaction between money and prices that results once money is allowed to be determined by the nominal dollar value of the needs of trade.

References

Aldrich, N. W. (1910) "The Work of the National Monetary Commission." Address before the Economic Club of New York. Washington: Government Printing Office.

Anderson, B. M. (1917) *The Value of Money*. New York: Macmillan.

———. ([1949] 1980) *Economics and the Public Welfare: A Financial and Economic History of the United States, 1914–1946*. Indianapolis: Liberty Fund.

Andrew, A. P. (1905) "Credit and the Value of Money." *Publications of the American Economic Association* 6 (1): 95–115.

———. (1908) "Substitutes for Cash in the Panic of 1907." *Quarterly Journal of Economics* 22 (4): 497–516.

Arnon, A. (2011) *Monetary Theory and Policy from Hume and Smith to Wicksell*. Cambridge: Cambridge University Press.

Bernanke, B. S. (1993) "The World on a Cross of Gold." Review of *Golden Fetters: The Gold Standard and the Great Depression, 1919–1939*, by B. Eichengreen. *Journal of Monetary Economics* 31 (2): 251–67.

Blaug, M. (1978) *Economic Theory in Retrospect*, 3rd ed. Cambridge: Cambridge University Press.

Board of Governors of the Federal Reserve System. (1924) *Tenth Annual Report*. Washington: Government Printing Office.

———. (1943) *Banking and Monetary Statistics*. Washington: Government Printing Office.

———. (1961) *The Federal Reserve Act as Amended through October 1961*. Washington: Government Printing Office.

Bopp, K. R. (1932) "Two Notes on the Federal Reserve System." *Journal of Political Economy* 40 (3): 379–91.

Bordo, M. (1992) "Gold Standard Theory." In P. Newman, M. Milgate, and J. Eatwell (eds.) *New Palgrave Dictionary of Money and Finance*, 267–71. London: Macmillan; and New York: The Stockton Press.

Bordo, M., Choudhri, E. U., and Schwartz, A. J. (2002) "Was Expansionary Monetary Policy Feasible during the Great Contraction? An Examination of the Gold Standard Constraint." *Explorations in Economic History* 39 (1): 1–28.

Bornemann, A. (1940) *J. Laurence Laughlin: Chapters in the Career of an Economist.* Washington: American Council on Public Affairs.

Bradford, F. A. (1935) "The Banking Act of 1935." *American Economic Review* 25 (4): 661–72.

Brunner, K., and Meltzer, A. H. (1968) "What Did We Learn from the Monetary Experience of the United States in the Great Depression?" *Canadian Journal of Economics* 2: 334–48.

Burgess, W. R. (1927) *The Reserve Banks and the Money Market.* New York: Harper.

———(ed.) ([1930] 1983) *Interpretations of Federal Reserve Policy in the Speeches and Writings of Benjamin Strong.* New York: Garland.

———. (1964) "Reflections on the Early Development of Open Market Policy." Federal Reserve Bank of New York *Monthly Review* 46: 219–26.

Cagan, P. (1965) *Determinants and Effects of Changes in the Stock of Money, 1875-1960.* New York: National Bureau of Economic Research and Columbia University Press.

Chandler, L. V. (1958) *Benjamin Strong, Central Banker.* Washington: Brookings Institution.

———. (1970) "Impacts of Theory on Policy: The Early Years of the Federal Reserve." In D. P. Eastburn (ed.) *Men, Money, and Policy: Essays in Honor of Karl R. Bopp*. Philadelphia: Federal Reserve Bank of Philadelphia.

Chipman, J. S. (1999) "Irving Fisher's Contributions to Economic Statistics and Econometrics." In H.-E. Loef and H. G. Monissen (eds.) *The Economics of Irving Fisher: Reviewing the Scientific Work of a Great Economist*. Northampton, MA: Edward Elgar.

Corry, B. A. (1962) *Money, Saving and Investment in English Economics 1800–1850*. New York: St. Martin's Press.

Currie, L. B. (1934) *The Supply and Control of Money in the United States*. Cambridge, MA: Harvard University Press.

De Cecco, M. (1992) "Gold Standard." In P. Newman, M. Milgate, and J. Eatwell (eds.) *New Palgrave Dictionary of Money and Finance*, 260–67. London: Macmillan.

Dorn, J. A. (2018) "Monetary Policy in an Uncertain World: The Case for Rules." *Cato Journal* 38 (1): 81–108.

Dowd, K. (1995) "Money and Banking: The American Experience." In C. F. Thies (ed.) *Money and Banking: The American Experience*, 1–30. Fairfax, VA: George Mason University Press.

Eccles, M. (1951) *Beckoning Frontiers*. New York: Alfred A. Knopf.

Edie, L. ([1932] 1983) "The Future of the Gold Standard." In Q. Wright (ed.) *Gold and Monetary Stabilization*, 108–30. New York: Garland.

Eichengreen, B. (1992) *Golden Fetters: The Gold Standard and the Great Depression, 1919–1939*. New York: Oxford University Press.

Fetter, F. W. (1965) *Development of British Monetary Orthodoxy 1797–1875*. Cambridge, MA: Harvard University Press.

Fisher, I. (1896) "Appreciation and Interest." *Publications of the American Economic Association* 11 (4): 331–442.

———. ([1911] 1913) *The Purchasing Power of Money*, 2nd ed. New York: Macmillan.

———. (1923) "The Business Cycle Largely a "Dance of the Dollar." *Journal of the American Statistical Association* 18 (144): 1024–28.

———. (1925) "Our Unstable Dollar and the So-Called Business Cycle." *Journal of the American Statistical Association* 20 (150): 179–202.

———. (1926) "A Statistical Relation between Unemployment and Price Changes." *International Labour Review* 13 (6): 785–92.

Friedman, M., and Schwartz, A. J. (1963) *A Monetary History of the United States 1867–1960*. Princeton, NJ: Princeton University Press for the National Bureau of Economic Research.

Fullarton, J. (1844) *On the Regulation of Currencies*. London: John Murray.

Girton, L. (1974) "SDR Creation and the Real-Bills Doctrine." *Southern Economic Journal* 41 (1): 57–61.

Girton, L., and Roper, D. (1978) "J. Laurence Laughlin and the Quantity Theory of Money." *Journal of Political Economy* 86 (4): 599–625.

Glasner, D. (2016) "Golden Misconceptions." *Uneasy Money* blog (December 25). https://uneasymoney.com/2016/12/.

Graham, F. D. (1930) *Exchange, Prices, and Production in Hyperinflation: Germany 1920–1923*. Princeton, NJ: Princeton University Press.

Hardy, C. O. (1932) *Credit Policies of the Federal Reserve System*. Washington: Brookings Institution.

Hepburn, A. B. (1924) *A History of Currency in the United States*. New York: Macmillan.

Hetzel, R. (1985) "The Rules versus Discretion Debate over Monetary Policy in the 1920s." Federal Reserve Bank of Richmond *Economic Review* 71 (6): 3–14.

———. (2008) *The Monetary Policy of the Federal Reserve*. Cambridge: Cambridge University Press.

Humphrey, T. M. (1980) "Eliminating Runaway Inflation: Lessons from the German Hyperinflation." Federal Reserve Bank of Richmond *Economic Review* 66 (4): 3–7.

———. (1982) "The Real Bills Doctrine." Federal Reserve Bank of Richmond *Economic Review* 68 (5): 3–13.

———. (2001) "The Choice of a Monetary Policy Framework: Lessons from the 1920s." *Cato Journal* 21 (2): 285–313.

Jastram, R. (1977) *The Golden Constant in English and American Experience, 1560–1976*. New York: John Wiley.

Johnson, G. G. (1939) *The Treasury and Monetary Policies, 1933–1938*. Cambridge, MA: Harvard University Press.

Kemmerer, E. W. (1907) *Money and Credit Instruments in Their Relation to General Prices*. New York: Henry Holt.

Kettl, D. F. (1986) *Leadership at the Fed*. New Haven, CT: Yale University Press.

King, P. (1804) *Thoughts on the Effects of the Bank Restrictions*, 2nd ed. London: Taylor.

Laidler, D. (1981) "Adam Smith as a Monetary Economist." *Canadian Journal of Economics* 14 (2): 185–200.

———. (1984) "Misconceptions about the Real Bills Doctrine: A Comment on Sargent and Wallace." *Journal of Political Economy* 92 (1): 149–155.

———. (1999) *Fabricating the Keynesian Revolution: Studies of the Inter-War Literature on Money, the Cycle, and Unemployment*. Cambridge: Cambridge University Press.

Laughlin, J. L. (1907) "Currency Reform." *Journal of Political Economy* 15 (10): 603–10.

Law, J. ([1705] 1720) *Money and Trade Considered: With a Proposal for Supplying the Nation with Money,* 2nd ed. Edinburgh: Andrew Anderson.

McCulloch, J. H. (1986) "Bank Regulation and Deposit Insurance." *Journal of Business* 59 (1): 79–85.

———. (1994) "The Crime of 1834." In George Edward Durell Foundation (ed.) *Money and Banking, the American Experience.* Fairfax, VA: George Mason University Press.

Meltzer, A. H. (1976) "Monetary and Other Explanations of the Start of the Great Depression." *Journal of Monetary Economics* 2 (4): 455–71.

———. (1997) "New Procedures, New Problems, 1923–29." Unpublished manuscript, Carnegie Mellon University (May).

———. (2003) *A History of the Federal Reserve System, 1913–1951.* Chicago: University of Chicago Press.

Miller, A. C. (1935a) "Responsibility for Federal Reserve Policies, 1927–29." *American Economic Review* 25 (3): 442–57.

———. (1935b) "The Banking Bill Considered in the Light of 1927–29." Statement released on June 24. In "Statements and Speeches of Adolph C. Miller." Available at https://fraser.stlouisfed.org /title/457.

Mints, L. W. (1945) *A History of Banking Theory in Great Britain and the United States.* Chicago: University of Chicago Press.

———. (1950) *Monetary Policy for a Competitive Society.* New York: McGraw-Hill.

———. (1951) "Monetary Policy and Stabilization." *American Economic Review* 41 (2): 188–93.

Newcomb, S. (1885) *Principles of Political Economy.* New York: Harper.

Norton, J. P. (1902) *Statistical Studies in the New York Money Market.* New York: Macmillan.

Patinkin, D. (1951) "Price Flexibility and Full Employment." In *Readings in Monetary Theory,* 252–83. New York: Blakiston.

Persons, W. M. (1908) "The Quantity Theory as Tested by Kemmerer." *Quarterly Journal of Economics* 22 (2): 274–89.

———. (1911) "Fisher's The Purchasing Power of Money." Review. *Publications of the American Statistical Association* 12 (69): 818–29.

Pigou, A. C. (1951) "Economic Progress in a Stable Environment." In *Readings in Monetary Theory,* 241–51. New York: Blakiston.

Reed, H. L. (1930) *Federal Reserve Policy, 1921–1930.* New York: McGraw-Hill.

Ricardo, D. ([1810–1811] 1951) "Notes on Bentham's 'Sur Les Prix.'" In P. Sraffa (ed.) *The Works and Correspondence of David Ricardo,* Vol. III. Cambridge: Cambridge University Press.

———. ([1821] 1852) "Principles of Political Economy and Taxation." In J. R. McCulloch (ed.) *The Works of David Ricardo,* 3rd ed. London: John Murray.

Richardson, G., Komai, A., and Gou, M. (2013) "The Banking Act of 1935." Available at http://www.federalreservehistory.org (November 22).

Riefler, W. W. (1930) *Money Rates and Money Markets in the United States.* New York: Harper.

Robbins, L. C. (1968) *The Theory of Economic Development in the History of Economic Thought.* New York: St. Martin's Press.

Sandilands, R. (1990) *The Life and Political Economy of Lauchlin Currie: New Dealer, Presidential Advisor and Development Economist.* London and Durham, NC: Duke University Press.

Sargent, T. J. (1979) *Macroeconomic Theory*. New York: Academic Press.

Sargent, T. J., and Wallace, N. (1982) "The Real-Bills Doctrine versus the Quantity Theory: A Reconsideration." *Journal of Political Economy* 90 (6): 1212–36.

Schumpeter, J. A. (1954) *History of Economic Analysis*. London: George Allen & Unwin.

Skaggs, N. T. (2010) "Less Than an Ideal Type: Varieties of Real Bills Doctrines." In R. Leeson (ed.) *David Laidler's Contributions to Economics*. New York: Palgrave Macmillan.

Selgin, G. (2017) *Money: Free and Unfree*. Washington: Cato Institute.

Seligman, E. R. A., ed. (1908) *The Currency Problems and the Present Financial Situation: A Series of Addresses Delivered at Columbia University, 1907–1908*. New York: Columbia University Press.

Smith, A. ([1776] 1937) *An Inquiry into the Nature and Causes of the Wealth of Nations*. New York: Random House.

Snyder, C. (1924) "New Measures in the Equation of Exchange." *American Economic Review* 14 (4): 699–713.

Sumner, S. (2016) *The Midas Paradox: Financial Markets, Government Policy Shocks, and the Great Depression*. Oakland, CA: The Independent Institute.

Temin, P. (1989) *Lessons from the Great Depression*. Cambridge, MA: MIT Press.

———. (1994) "The Great Depression." National Bureau of Economic Research (NBER) Historical Paper No. 62. Cambridge, MA: NBER.

Thornton, H. ([1802] 1939) *An Enquiry into the Nature and Effects of the Paper Credit of Great Britain*. Edited with an introduction by F. A. Hayek. New York: Rinehart.

Timberlake, R. H. (1993) *Monetary Policy in the United States: An Institutional and Intellectual History.* Chicago: University of Chicago Press and Cato Institute.

―――. (2007) "Gold Standards and the Real Bills Doctrine in U.S. Monetary Policy." The *Independent Review* 11 (3): 325–54.

―――. (2013) *Constitutional Money: A Review of the Supreme Court's Monetary Decisions.* New York: Cambridge University Press and Cato Institute.

U.S. Census Bureau (1960) *Historical Statistics of the United States, Colonial Times to 1957.* Washington: Government Printing Office.

U. S. Congress (1927) "Stabilization: Hearings before the Committee on Banking and Currency, House of Representatives, Sixty-Ninth Congress, First Session, on H. R. 7895." Washington: Government Printing Office.

―――. (1929) "Stabilization: Hearings before the Committee on Banking and Currency, House of Representatives, Seventieth Congress, First Session, on H. R. 11806 (Superseding H. R. 7895, Sixty-Ninth Congress)." Washington: Government Printing Office.

U.S. Department of the Treasury (1931) "Annual Report of the Secretary of the Treasury on the State of the Finances for Fiscal Year ended June 30, 1931." Washington: Government Printing Office.

―――. (1932) "Annual Report of the Secretary of the Treasury on the State of the Finances for Fiscal Year ended June 30, 1932." Washington: Government Printing Office.

Viner, J. (1936) "Recent Legislation and the Banking Situation." *American Economic Review* 26 (1) (supplement): 106–19.

―――. ([1937] 1965) *Studies in the Theory of International Trade.* New York: Augustus Kelley.

Warburton, C. (1966) *Depression, Inflation, and Monetary Policy, Selected Papers, 1945–1953*. Baltimore, MD: Johns Hopkins University Press.

West, R. C. (1977) *Banking Reform and the Federal Reserve, 1863–1923*. Ithaca, NY: Cornell University Press.

Wheelock, D. C. (1991) *The Strategy and Consistency of Federal Reserve Monetary Policy, 1924–1933*. Cambridge: Cambridge University Press.

———. (1998) "Monetary Policy in the Great Depression and Beyond: The Sources of the Fed's Inflation Bias." In M. Wheeler (ed.) *The Economics of the Great Depression*. Kalamazoo, MI: W. E. Upjohn Institute for Employment Research.

White, H. (1935) *Money and Banking*. Revised and enlarged by C. Tippets and L. Froman. Boston: Ginn and Co.

White, L. H. (1997) "Banking School, Currency School, Free Banking School." In D. Glasner (ed.) *Business Cycles and Depressions: An Encyclopedia*. New York: Garland Publishing.

———. (2008) "Is the Gold Standard Still the Gold Standard among Monetary Systems?" Cato Institute Briefing Paper No. 100 (February 8).

———. (2012) *The Clash of Economic Ideas, the Great Policy Debates of the Last Hundred Years*. New York: Cambridge University Press.

———. (2016) "Did the Gold Standard Fail: A Response to David Glasner." *Alt-M* blog (October 6).

Wicker, E. (1966) *Federal Reserve Monetary Policy, 1917–1933*. New York: Random House.

Wicksell, K. (1898) *Interest and Prices*. Trans. R. F. Khan. Reprint Kelley. New York. 1965

Williams, J. H. (1936) "The Banking Act of 1935." *American Economic Review* 26 (1) (supplement): 95–105.

Willis, H. P. (1915) *The Federal Reserve*. New York: Doubleday and Page.

Wood, J. H. (2015) *Central Banking in a Democracy: The Federal Reserve and Its Alternatives*. New York: Routledge.

Working, H. (1923) "Prices and the Quantity of the Circulating Medium, 1890–1921." *Quarterly Journal of Economics* 37 (2): 228–56.

———. (1926) "Bank Deposits as a Forecaster of the General Wholesale Price Level." *Review of Economics and Statistics* 8 (3): 120–33.

Wright, Q., ed. ([1932] 1983) *Gold and Monetary Stabilization*. New York: Garland.

Yeager, L. (1966) *International Monetary Relations: Theory, History, and Policy*. New York: Harper and Row.

Yohe, W. P. (1990) "The Intellectual Milieu at the Federal Reserve Board in the 1920s." *History of Political Economy* 22 (3): 465–88.

Index

speculation and, 45–47, 59–60,
75–76, 79–81, 125–27
theories of, 167
U.S. Treasury and, 45–47, 141, 163–65
Fetter, F. W., 9n1, 9n2, 19n10
Fisher Effect, 21n12
Fisher, Irving, 57–58, 60–62, 64–67, 104
quantity theoretic cycle model, 67
FOMC. *See* Federal Open Market
Committee
fractional reserve banking, 38, 60
due bills, post notes, and, 28n1
Free Banking School, 20n11
Friedman, Milton, 167, 170n2, 171–72
Fullarton, John, 18–19
fungibility of credit, 48

German hyperinflation, 21–25
Girton, Lance, 23–24
Glass, Carter, 33, 37, 78, 110, 139, 143–45
Glass-Steagall Act, 99, 127
gold. *See also* devaluation of gold dollar;
gold standard
certificates, 84, 112, 117, 127–28,
132, 161
clauses, 128, 132–33, 135
currencies, 1, 3–4, 119–20
imports pre–World War II, 149
ingots, 130–31
money stock and, 6–7, 94, 120,
130–31, 149
price of, 4–5, 7, 12n5, 66–67, 123,
128–29, 132, 135, 140
recall of, 128–37
reserves of U.S. Treasury, 41–42, 116,
149, 162
supply of, 19n10, 94
Gold and Monetary Stabilization, 87–100
Gold Reserve Act, 129–37
Supreme Court cases about, 132–37
gold standard, xvii–xviii, 3–5, 6–8,
12, 19n10, 164. *See also* Federal
Reserve System: gold standard and
abandonment of, 94, 112, 127–30,
165, 170–73
critics of, 87, 118, 120–23

devaluations under, 136
Federal Reserve Act and, 94–95, 119–20
vs. gold currencies, 4, 123
goods and, 4
Great Contraction and, 115–23
managed vs. operational, 7–8, 66–67,
98–100, 169–71
price level stabilization and, 73–75,
104–5
Real Bills Doctrine and, 6, 70, 93–94,
172–73
Strong, Benjamin on, 73–78
in U.S. law, 4–5, 119–21, 128–37
World War I, and xvii, 69
goods
gold standard, and 4
production of, 3, 139
real bills and, 1–2, 15–16, 177–79
stockpiling of, 50
government securities, 38
as collateral for Federal Reserve
notes, 127–129
interest rates and, 174
as nonproductive credit, 45–46, 52
purchase program of 1932, 101–2, 125
Great Contraction and Depression, xvii–xix, 8, 56–57. *See
also* Federal Reserve System: Great
Contraction and Depression and
cause of, xviii
direct pressure and, 83–84, 126–28
gold standard and, 115–23
inflation and, 152–60
money stock during, xvii
Real Bills Doctrine and, 23, 56,
59–60, 139
reserve requirements and, 158–60
greenbacks, 38, 41–42, 131
Civil War and, 1, 28, 121
court cases about, 133–34
gross national product, xvii, 118–19

Haberler, Gottfried, 88
Hardy, Charles O., 102–9
Hepburn, A. Barton, 33–34
Hoover, Herbert, 125–26

supply and demand of money, 23–26,
  51
  gold standard and, 94–96
Supreme Court, 133–37
Thomas, Elmer, 144–46
  amendment to Agricultural Adjust-
    ment Act, 101–2, 128, 145n10
Thornton, Henry, 14–21
Treasury-fiscalist-spending theory, 167
Treasury (U.S.), 36–37, 41
  Federal Reserve System and, 45–47,
    140, 163–65
  gold reserves of, 41, 116–19, 149,
    162
  gold sterilization policy, 163–64
  recall of gold, 129–35, 161–63

unemployment, xvii
unit banks, 27
velocity of money
  during German hyperinflation,
    23
  money stock and, 173
  recessions and, 159
Viner, Jacob, 87–88, 165

Wallace, N., 2n3
Warburg, Paul, 34–35
Williams, John H., 97–100, 165
Willis, H. Parker, 20, 33, 78, 88–93
Working, Holbrook, 60, 63–66
World War I, xvii, 69–70
Wright, Quincy, 87–88

ABOUT THE AUTHORS

Thomas Humphrey was for 34 years a research economist at the Federal Reserve Bank of Richmond. He served as longtime editor of and contributor to the bank's flagship publications, successively, the *Monthly Review*, *Economic Review*, and *Economic Quarterly*. He has published several books, including *The Monetary Approach to the Balance of Payments, Exchange Rates, and World Inflation* (1982), coauthored with Robert E. Keleher; *Money, Banking and Inflation: Essays in the History of Monetary Thought* (1993); *Money, Exchange and Production: Further Essays in the History of Economic Thought* (1998); and *Essays on Inflation* (Fifth edition, 1986). He holds an MS degree from the University of Tennessee-Knoxville and a PhD from Tulane University.

Richard H. Timberlake is an emeritus professor of economics at the University of Georgia and an adjunct scholar at the Cato Institute. His research specialties are monetary policy and the history of central banking. He has had published approximately 48 articles analyzing monetary principles and policy in prominent economic journals, including some on the spontaneous emergence of private money. His most recent publications include *Constitutional Money: A Review of the Supreme Court's Monetary Decisions* (2013); *Monetary Policy in the United States: An Institutional and Intellectual History* (1993); and with Kevin Dowd, *Money and the Nation State: The Financial Revolution, Government, and the World Monetary System* (1998). He received his PhD in Economics from the University of Chicago in 1959.

ABOUT THE CATO INSTITUTE AND ITS CENTER FOR MONETARY AND FINANCIAL ALTERNATIVES

Founded in 1977, the Cato Institute is a public policy research foundation dedicated to broadening the parameters of policy debate to allow consideration of more options that are consistent with the principles of limited government, individual liberty, and peace.

The Institute is named for *Cato's Letters*, libertarian pamphlets that were widely read in the American colonies in the early 18th century and played a major role in laying the philosophical foundation for the American Revolution.

The Cato Institute undertakes an extensive publications program on the complete spectrum of policy issues. Books, monographs, and shorter studies are commissioned to examine the federal budget, Social Security, regulation, military spending, international trade, and myriad other issues. Major policy conferences are held throughout the year.

The Cato Institute's Center for Monetary and Financial Alternatives was founded in 2014 to assess the shortcomings of existing monetary and financial regulatory arrangements, and to discover and promote more stable and efficient alternatives.

In order to maintain its independence, the Cato Institute accepts no government funding. Contributions are received from foundations, corporations, and individuals, and other revenue is generated from the sale of publications. The Institute is a nonprofit, tax-exempt, educational foundation under Section 501(c)3 of the Internal Revenue Code.

Cato Institute
1000 Massachusetts Ave., N.W.
Washington, D.C. 20001
www.cato.org